LIORA FREEWIND

The Art of Loving Yourself

Building Lasting Confidence as a Woman

Contents

Preface

Self-love is not just a luxury—it is a necessity for living an empowered and fulfilling life. In a world that constantly challenges our worth and imposes unattainable standards, cultivating self-acceptance becomes an act of quiet rebellion. *The Art of Loving Yourself* is an invitation to every woman who has ever felt the weight of self-doubt or the sting of comparison to step into her power and embrace her authentic self.

This book explores the profound impact self-esteem has on every facet of life, from relationships to personal growth. It offers practical tools like journaling, affirmations, and mindfulness to help you build a resilient foundation of self-love. With each chapter, you will uncover the significance of internal validation, confront insecurities, and learn to reframe failures as opportunities for growth.

The journey of self-love is not linear, nor is it always easy. Yet, it is transformative. This book does not promise perfection but instead guides you toward celebrating your imperfections as essential elements of your uniqueness. Let this be your companion in redefining confidence, nurturing emotional healing, and ultimately, mastering the art of loving yourself.

Introduction

Every woman, at some point in her life, has grappled with the shadow of self-doubt. It might appear unexpectedly, whispering words of inadequacy as you prepare for a job interview or questioning your worthwhile you balance the demands of family life. Imagine if I told you that hidden within these moments of uncertainty is the power to transform that doubt into unshakeable confidence. Whether you're a young adult stepping into the workforce or a mother striving to nurture both yourself and your loved ones, this book is a journey toward discovering the self-assurance that already resides within you.

As you scroll through social media, it's easy to feel overwhelmed by images of seemingly perfect lives and flawless appearances curated by filters and careful highlights. These images can provoke feelings of insecurity, leading us to question our value and worth. But it's time to reclaim the narrative – to step away from the screen and embrace who we truly are, imperfections and all. This book acknowledges the unique challenges women face in building self-esteem and personal growth. Doing so seeks to make you feel understood and less alone on this transformative path.

In the pages ahead, be prepared to embark on a journey of empowerment and self-discovery. You will find practical strategies designed to help you navigate insecurities and nurture self-love. From journaling exercises that encourage reflective thinking to goal-setting techniques that provide direction, these tools aim to guide you toward becoming more confident and secure in who you are. It's not just about temporary boosts of confidence; it's about cultivating a mindset of lasting transformation, paving the way for a resilient and empowered you.

Imagine waking up each day with a renewed purpose, ready to face challenges head-on with courage and determination. With the right mindset and tools, every setback becomes a stepping stone toward personal growth and fulfillment. This book encourages you to adopt a growth mindset—a belief that changes, even those involving deeply ingrained patterns of self-doubt, are possible with effort and perseverance. As you turn each page, envision the possibilities of what you can achieve when guided by confidence and clarity.

The foundation of self-esteem begins with understanding its true essence. It's not merely about possessing confidence; it's deeply intertwined with our beliefs and feelings about ourselves. Self-esteem can fluctuate based on the tapestry of life experiences and events, sometimes influencing how we perceive our value. Distinguishing between self-esteem and self-confidence is crucial as they are interrelated yet distinct concepts. High self-esteem contributes positively to mental health and overall satisfaction in life, acting as a pillar of resilience against life's challenges.

In your journey through these chapters, you will delve into the importance of self-esteem and why it's imperative for women to reclaim their narratives, prioritizing emotional well-being. You will encounter testimonies from women who have transformed their lives by embracing their self-worth. You'll also explore the concept of genuine versus conditional self-esteem—understanding that while genuine self-esteem stems from self-acceptance, conditional self-esteem often relies on external validation and achievements.

Recognizing your unique strengths and accomplishments is an integral part of building a strong foundation for self-esteem. Reflective exercises prompt you to list and value your strengths, creating an inventory that celebrates both personal and professional accomplishments. Through shared experiences and supportive environments, you will see how other women have celebrated their victories, motivating you to acknowledge and celebrate yours without reservation.

Distinguishing between internal and external validation plays a pivotal role in shaping one's self-esteem. Internal validation comes from recognizing and accepting oneself, contributing to stability irrespective of external opinions. Meanwhile, external validation involves societal approval and feedback. This book guides you in finding a harmonious relationship between the two, providing tips on cultivating strong internal validation practices while maintaining healthy social feedback.

Self-talk is another powerful tool in shaping self-image and self-esteem. You'll learn how to tune into your internal dialogue, identify its tone and content, and shift from negative to positive self-talk. Through practical strategies like affirmations and realigning inner dialogue, you'll discover how changing your self-talk can enhance self-worth and confidence.

Overcoming societal pressures and expectations is a journey in itself. Recognizing these pressures and addressing the emotional toll they impose is essential for fostering self-acceptance. By exploring diverse narratives and celebrating authenticity, you'll gain inspiration to break free from conventional expectations and prioritize your unique self.

This book invites educators, mentors, counsellors, and anyone supporting women in their journey toward self-confidence to recommend it as a resource for personal development. The stories, strategies, and testimonies shared within these pages serve as motivational resources, encouraging women to redefine their self-worth and embrace authentic lives.

As you immerse yourself in this journey of self-discovery, remember that the journey doesn't end with understanding—it thrives on action and continual growth. Embrace the tools and insights offered in this book, and with each step forward, know that you are capable of transforming self-doubt into a beacon of unshakeable confidence. Here's to the journey of becoming the confident, empowered woman you're destined to be.

Building the Foundation of Self-Esteem

Building the foundation of self-esteem involves understanding its significance and the components that contribute to a healthy sense of self-worth. Self-esteem is not simply an abstract concept; it is a crucial aspect of our identity that defines how we view ourselves and our place in the world. This chapter delves into the profound impact self-esteem has on mental health, relationships, and personal fulfillment. By exploring various facets of self-esteem, we can appreciate its role as a cornerstone of psychological resilience. As you navigate this chapter, you'll uncover insights into the intrinsic value of recognizing your worth and the empowering effect it has on your life journey.

This chapter aims to provide a comprehensive exploration of self-esteem, distinguishing it from similar concepts like self-confidence while debunking common misconceptions. The discussions will include how self-esteem impacts mental health, adaptation to life's challenges, and the idea that it is a dynamic trait that can be nurtured over time. Readers will be guided through strategies to identify personal strengths, celebrate accomplishments, and create internal feedback loops that reinforce self-worth. Practical exercises and reflective techniques are presented to aid in nurturing self-esteem, highlighting the importance of mindful practices and support networks. This narrative offers tools for both personal growth and professional guidance, making it especially relevant for women seeking empowerment, individuals recovering from past traumas, and mentors supporting others in their developmental journeys.

Understanding What Self-Esteem Truly Means

Self-esteem is a fundamental component of our psychological makeup, playing a critical role in shaping how we perceive ourselves and interact with the world. At its core, self-esteem refers to one's overall sense of self-worth or personal value. It is an internal reflection of how much we appreciate and accept ourselves as worthwhile individuals. This concept is not only about feeling good about oneself but encompasses the deeper cognitive and emotional appraisals that we hold about our inherent worthiness.

To fully grasp the significance of self-esteem, it's important to differentiate it from concepts often mistakenly used interchangeably with it, such as self-confidence. Self-esteem is deeply rooted in our beliefs about our value and worth as a person. It tends to be more stable over time and less influenced by external circumstances. In contrast, self-confidence revolves around the trust we have in our abilities and competencies. It is situational, fluctuating based on the context or task at hand. For instance, a person may feel highly confident when giving presentations due to their skills and experience but might have low self-esteem if they hold negative beliefs about their overall worth. Recognizing this distinction highlights how individuals with high self-confidence can still struggle with low self-esteem, impacting their mental health and overall life satisfaction.

The importance of healthy self-esteem cannot be overstated. It serves as a foundation for mental health, enabling individuals to navigate life's challenges resiliently. Those with positive self-esteem are generally more adaptable and open to new experiences, allowing them to seize opportunities more effectively. They possess a grounded sense of identity and acceptance, which empowers them to take risks and pursue goals without the paralyzing fear of failure or rejection. The advantages extend to various facets of life, including improved relationships, career satisfaction, and a greater inclination toward creativity and innovation, as individuals with a robust sense of self-worth are typically more willing to engage with the world meaningfully.

Despite these benefits, self-esteem is often misunderstood due to prevalent myths. One common misconception is that self-esteem is fixed from childhood and cannot be changed. However, research suggests that self-esteem is malleable and can be developed or strengthened throughout life. Personal experiences, feedback from others, and conscious efforts to change self-perception can significantly influence self-esteem levels. Approaches such as positive affirmations, therapy, and practicing self-compassion can help nurture and elevate self-worth over time.

Another myth equates high self-esteem with arrogance or excessive pride. While arrogant behaviour centers around an inflated sense of superiority over others, healthy self-esteem involves recognizing one's own value without comparing oneself to others. People with balanced self-esteem demonstrate humility, acknowledging both strengths and weaknesses, which enables them to grow and collaborate without feeling threatened or diminished by others' successes. This understanding dispels fears that enhancing self-esteem might lead to egocentric behaviours.

Moreover, fostering self-esteem requires awareness and intentional practice. It's essential to move beyond societal definitions of success, which often measure worth through accomplishments, wealth, or status. Instead, true self-esteem arises from aligning with personal values and finding intrinsic satisfaction in being authentically oneself. It involves accepting imperfections, celebrating individuality, and living a life congruent with one's own principles rather than external expectations.

The journey to building and maintaining healthy self-esteem begins with introspection. Individuals are encouraged to examine their thoughts and beliefs about themselves, identifying areas where negativity undermines self-worth. By challenging these beliefs and replacing them with more realistic and supportive narratives, they can strengthen their esteem. Furthermore, surrounding oneself with supportive and encouraging people who reinforce one's values can make a significant difference in this process.

Additionally, practices such as mindfulness and gratitude can enhance self-esteem by fostering a greater appreciation for one's life and accomplishments. Mindfulness helps individuals become more aware of their thoughts and recognize patterns damaging to self-esteem, while gratitude shifts focus from perceived shortcomings to the positives, reinforcing a sense of worthiness and contentment.

Identifying Personal Strengths and Accomplishments

In a world bustling with comparisons and constant change, recognizing and valuing one's unique strengths and successes are vital in building the foundation of self-esteem. This involves engaging in reflective exercises that enable individuals to chart their journey, appreciate their individuality, and create an internal feedback loop that fosters confidence.

Reflective exercises serve as tools for introspection, prompting individuals to take inventory of their strengths and achievements. One effective approach is the use of guided activities that encourage people to write down personal accomplishments and identify skills or attributes that have contributed to these successes. These exercises not only help in understanding what one excels at but also illuminate areas where these strengths have been applied effectively. Through this practice, individuals can develop a clearer picture of their capabilities, leading to increased self-awareness and motivation. As individuals enumerate their strengths and achievements, they may begin to recognize patterns in the areas where they excel, providing insights into how these strengths can be leveraged in other aspects of life.

Revisiting milestones through a 'success journal' can further bolster one's self-esteem by framing past achievements as stepping stones for future endeavours. This journal becomes a tangible record of triumphs, big and small, serving as a reminder of what has already been accomplished. Revisiting these milestones, especially during times of doubt or low confidence, can provide reassurance and renew motivation. The act of documenting achievements allows individuals to track progress over time, offering a comprehensive view of their growth and learning curve. This process emphasizes that each success, regardless of size, is a cumulative contribution to personal development and can be used as a motivational tool for setting new goals and overcoming challenges.

Additionally, appreciating one's uniqueness is essential, considering how societal narratives often downplay individual strengths. Each person possesses distinct qualities that make them valuable and different from others. Embracing this individuality means acknowledging that society's standards do not define one's worth; instead, personal value is rooted in authenticity and the distinctive combination of skills and traits each person brings to the table. It is crucial to remember that societal pressures can sometimes cause individuals to overlook their strengths, making it important to consciously affirm and celebrate personal achievements and characteristics that set one apart. By doing so, individuals learn to appreciate their contributions to various spheres of life, leading to enhanced self-esteem and fulfillment.

Creating a positive feedback loop is another powerful strategy to cement internal validation. This concept revolves around using internal resources—personal reflections and reminders of past successes—to establish a baseline of confidence from which further achievements can be pursued. When individuals acknowledge their abilities and successes internally, they cultivate resilience against external criticisms or failures. This self-reinforcing mechanism encourages continuous personal growth and achievement as individuals draw strength and motivation from within. To implement a positive feedback loop effectively, one might start by regularly reviewing personal achievements and reflecting on the intrinsic satisfaction derived from these experiences. Over time, this solidifies a cycle of confidence-building and skill-enhancement that propels individuals toward even greater accomplishments, ultimately strengthening their sense of self-worth.

Distinguishing Between Internal and External Validation

Within the intricate tapestry of self-esteem, validation forms a crucial thread that influences how individuals perceive themselves and their worth. Understanding the dynamics between internal and external validation offers pathways to fostering more robust self-esteem, particularly for those navigating life's complexities.

Internal validation is the cornerstone of strong self-esteem, characterized by the recognition and acceptance of one's intrinsic value. It involves looking inward to acknowledge personal achievements, desires, and emotions without the need for outside approval. An individual who achieves internal validation develops resilience against external judgments and feels more grounded in their identity. This form of validation can be nurtured through mindfulness practices and reflective exercises that encourage an honest appraisal of one's strengths and weaknesses. As an inward-focused practice, it empowers individuals to embrace authenticity, cultivating a sense of fulfillment derived from personal growth and self-acceptance.

In contrast, external validation originates from societal feedback, often impacting self-worth as individuals look to others for affirmation. Societal norms play a significant role in shaping perceptions of worthiness, leading many to equate outside validation with value. While receiving praise and acknowledgement from others can bolster confidence temporarily, an over-reliance can result in instability. When self-esteem is heavily dependent on external sources, individuals may become vulnerable to manipulation, criticism, and rejection. This reliance fosters a cycle where self-worth fluctuates based on external opinions rather than inner truths. It highlights the importance of recognizing when an external influence begins to undermine one's core beliefs and self-view. The journey toward healthy self-esteem entails understanding and managing how these external forces impact personal perception.

Balancing internal and external validation is vital for achieving stable self-esteem. Cultivating a balance means welcoming constructive feedback while not letting it define self-worth. The ability to discern which external affirmations to integrate and which to question requires critical self-awareness. Healthy validation involves being open to feedback that facilitates growth while remaining anchored in one's values and self-assessment. One should aim to maintain a foundation of internal validation, using external insights as tools for development rather than determinants of value. Developing this balance can foster emotional stability and enhance individual resilience against societal pressures. Providing guidelines for maintaining this balance includes setting boundaries on what external feedback is allowed to influence your self-perception and practicing consistent self-reflection to remain aligned with personal values.

Creating a personal validation journal is a practical tool for exploring and balancing these forms of validation. This journal serves as a repository for recording experiences of both internal and external validation, allowing individuals to reflect on how different encounters affect their self-esteem. By regularly documenting thoughts, feelings, and reactions to various validation experiences, individuals can identify patterns that contribute to or detract from their self-worth. Reflective journaling helps in distinguishing situations where external input was beneficial or where it might have undermined intrinsic confidence. Over time, such reflection aids in developing strategies to emphasize internal validation, reinforcing self-belief, and selectively valuing external feedback. Guidelines for keeping a journal include employing prompts such as "What internal qualities do I appreciate about myself today?" or "How did someone else's opinion affect me, and why?"

For women seeking to overcome insecurity, developing a strong base of internal validation is particularly empowering. Women often face heightened societal pressures to conform to specific standards, which underscores the necessity of nurturing self-validation. When internal validation is prioritized, women are better equipped to navigate the external demands they encounter in personal and professional realms. They can make empowered choices unencumbered by the need for external endorsement. Similarly, individuals recovering from past trauma may find solace in reinforcing internal validation and discovering renewed strength and self-respect as they heal. Educators, mentors, and counselors can adopt these concepts to support their clients, offering motivational resources that emphasize the importance of self-recognition and reducing dependency on external validation.

Exploring How Self-Talk Affects Self-Image

Understanding the nuances of self-talk is essential for building a foundation of self-esteem. At its core, self-talk refers to the internal dialogue that occurs within our minds every day.

It's this powerful and often unconscious process that plays a significant role in shaping our self-worth and psychological well-being. When we engage in positive self-talk, we reinforce our self-esteem, whereas negative self-talk can diminish it. For many women facing insecurities or recovering from past traumas, being aware of this internal dialogue can be the first step toward empowerment.

Negative self-talk takes on various forms. It might manifest as critical thoughts about one's abilities, appearance, or worth. This kind of internal discourse tends to breed self-doubt, which can erode confidence over time. Imagine someone who constantly thinks, "I'm not good enough" or "I always fail." These thoughts can become self-fulfilling prophecies, leading the individual to approach challenges with hesitation or avoid them altogether. On the contrary, positive self-talk such as "I am capable" or "I can overcome challenges" serves as a booster, encouraging resilience and fostering a more robust self-image.

The impact of self-talk on self-image cannot be overstated. Positive affirmations are known to enhance how individuals perceive themselves. They reinforce a sense of competence and value, crucial components of healthy self-esteem. Conversely, continual exposure to negative self-statements can obscure one's perception, making them doubt their capabilities and self-worth. The correlation between effective self-talk and im-proved cognitive performance is well-documented in research, underscoring its influence (Kim et al., 2021).

Recognizing this power allows us to change the narrative of our internal dialogue. Transitioning from negative to positive self-talk requires conscious effort and dedication. Simple yet intentional practices, such as daily affirmations, can facilitate this shift. Consider starting each day by vocalizing positive statements like "I am worthy" or "I embrace challenges as opportunities to grow." Over time, these affirmations can reshape thought patterns, allowing positivity to replace detrimental self-criticism.

To make this transformation more tangible, creating a self-talk worksheet can be an instrumental tool. This practice involves documenting instances of self-talk throughout the day and noting emotions and triggers associated with these dialogues. By doing so, patterns emerge, highlighting specific situations or environments that provoke negative thoughts. With this awareness, you can consciously redirect your self-talk, aiming for encouraging and supportive language.

Here are some guidelines for crafting a self-talk worksheet: Start by dedicating a section to logging challenging moments where negative self-talk occurred. Note the context—what was happening around you, how you felt, and what precisely ran through your mind. In another section, document the positive counter-statements you want to adopt. For example, if you often think, "I always mess up," your replacement could be, "I learn from my mistakes and grow stronger." Revisit this worksheet regularly, refining your approach as you gain insight into your inner dialogue.

Moreover, it's crucial to understand that replacing entrenched negative talk isn't an overnight endeavour. It demands persistence and patience. Nonetheless, the potential benefits—enhanced self-esteem, better emotional health, and increased motivation—are well worth the effort. In transforming our internal conversations, we take control of our narratives, setting the stage for personal growth and fulfillment.

However, while striving for positivity, it's also important to remain grounded. Effective self-talk reflects reality; it doesn't ignore challenges but frames them constructively. Instead of deluding oneself with unrealistic affirmations, aim for balanced optimism. Acknowledge difficulties, yet affirm your capability to overcome them. This realistic approach not only supports self-esteem but also equips individuals with the resilience needed to navigate life's ups and downs.

Overcoming Societal Pressures and Expectations

Recognizing societal pressures is the first step in understanding how they shape our perceptions of self-worth. From early childhood, individuals are exposed to societal standards and ideals that often set unrealistic expectations. These pressures manifest through various channels, including media, peer influences, and cultural norms. The bombardment of images and messages can subtly influence beliefs about body image, success, and happiness, leading many to internalize these ideals as benchmarks for personal value. Recognizing the origins of these pressures allows individuals to critically assess their impact on self-esteem, offering a path to deconstruct harmful beliefs.

The pressure to conform often results in an emotional toll that can be both exhausting and damaging. Many feel compelled to mold themselves to fit societal molds while sacrificing authenticity in the process. Stories abound of women who embarked on quests for liberation, learning to reject conformity to embrace their true selves. In doing so, they discovered not only personal freedom but also a newfound resilience. These narratives serve as powerful reminders that striving for societal approval can lead to feelings of inadequacy and anxiety. Conversely, choosing authenticity over approval can foster inner strength and self-acceptance.

Building resilience against societal pressure involves reinforcing personal values and seeking support from nurturing communities. Resilience, defined as the ability to adapt well in the face of adversity (Liu et al., 2021), plays a crucial role here. It enables individuals to maintain psychological well-being despite external stressors. Strategies such as setting personal goals aligned with one's core values and practicing self-care enhance resilience. Additionally, surrounding oneself with supportive people who affirm personal worth can buffer against negative impacts. Social support acts as a protective factor, helping individuals to form a positive self-image and promote self-esteem (Liu et al., 2021).

Celebrating real-life authenticity means acknowledging and valuing the diversity of human experience. Sharing stories of individuals who have challenged conventional norms highlights the richness of authentic living. These narratives inspire others to embrace their genuine selves in a world that often champions uniformity. For instance, consider the tales of those who defy traditional career paths or challenge stereotypes about beauty and success. By celebrating these diverse experiences, we create a culture of acceptance and encouragement, promoting self-confidence and authentic expression.

Incorporating practices that build resilience plays a vital role in countering societal pressures. Individuals can cultivate resilience by engaging in activities that nurture physical, emotional, and mental health, such as exercise and meditation (<i>Coping with Peer Pressure: Building Resilience & Self-Confidence | Therapy for Young Adults | Therapy for Colorado</i>, n.d.). Prioritizing self-compassion and kindness further strengthens resilience, helping individuals navigate challenges without succumbing to external pressures. As resilience grows, so does one's capacity to uphold personal values amidst societal demands.

To truly empower readers, this section provides practical strategies for building resilience. Begin by identifying and affirming core personal values. This involves reflecting on what genuinely matters, untainted by societal expectations. Engaging in exercises like writing down personal principles or creating vision boards helps solidify these values. Furthermore, breaking personal goals into smaller achievable steps can make them manageable, enhancing focus and motivation. Each small victory reinforces resilience, boosting confidence and promoting a sense of accomplishment when facing societal pressures.

Surrounding oneself with a supportive community is another key strategy. Positive relationships provide a safe space for growth and self-expression, shielding against negative societal messages. Creating a network of friends, family, or mentors who respect and affirm individual values fosters a sense of belonging. This social support system offers encouragement during challenges and celebrates successes, reinforcing self-esteem and authenticity (Liu et al., 2021). Actively seeking environments that value diversity and individuality enriches this communal support, providing inspiration through shared experiences and perspectives.

Sharing and celebrating real-life stories that defy norms encourages authenticity. These narratives showcase the bravery of individuals who chose to live authentically despite societal pressures. Their journeys inspire others to pursue personal truths, highlighting the joy and fulfillment that authenticity brings. Embracing one's unique identity not only enhances self-esteem but also paves the way for others to do the same. By shining a light on diverse experiences, society evolves toward greater acceptance and appreciation of individuality, empowering more people to break free from conformist pressures.

Concluding Thoughts

In this chapter, we have explored the foundation of self-esteem, highlighting its significance and various components. It has been emphasized that true self-esteem is more than just a fleeting sense of confidence; it is deeply rooted in our beliefs about our values and worth as individuals. By differentiating self-esteem from self-confidence, we've gained insights into how one's sense of self-worth can remain stable even when facing life's challenges. Through understanding myths surrounding self-esteem, such as it being fixed or equated with arrogance, we've learned that our self-perception is malleable and can be nurtured through deliberate practices like positive affirmations and mindfulness.

For women seeking guidance and support and for those overcoming past traumas, nurturing self-esteem is both empowering and uplifting. Building a strong base requires introspection and identifying personal strengths, thereby realizing intrinsic value beyond societal expectations. As covered in the chapter, recognizing and appreciating one's uniqueness against external pressures helps build resilience. Moreover, educators, mentors, and counsellors can leverage these insights to foster environments where women feel supported and encouraged. Through intentional practice, individuals can create a solid foundation of self-esteem, embrace authenticity, and navigate life confidently and resiliently.

Confronting Insecurities and Negative Thoughts

Confronting insecurities and negative thoughts is a journey many women undertake, striving to transform self-doubt into growth. It's about recognizing the inner battles unique to each individual yet universally shared among us. Insecurities often stem from deep-seated fears or past experiences that shape our perceptions of ourselves. These feelings can cloud judgment and stifle potential, but they also present opportunities for introspection and positive change. Understanding these emotions involves more than mere acknowledgment; it requires courage to face them head-on. This confrontation, while challenging, sets the stage for profound personal development by opening pathways for healing and resilience.

Within this chapter, readers will explore diverse strategies designed to dismantle the barriers posed by insecurities. The discussion delves into identifying emotional triggers that exacerbate feelings of inadequacy, providing insight into their origins. Such awareness becomes a tool for empowerment, enabling individuals to respond thoughtfully rather than react impulsively. Readers will also discover practical methods like journaling to track and analyze patterns of thought, encouraging clarity and control over one's emotional landscape.

Breaking down harmful self-talk forms another cornerstone of the chapter, teaching how to replace negativity with affirmations that foster self-worth and strength. Additionally, the chapter highlights the importance of community and shared experiences, illustrating how collective support nurtures growth. Through embracing vulnerability and openness, individuals create networks that uplift and inspire, reminding them they're not alone in this quest for self-improvement. Each section aims to equip women, those healing from trauma, and mentors guiding others with tangible tools for navigating their personal journeys toward confidence and fulfillment.

Recognizing Common Patterns of Insecurity

When confronting insecurities and negative thoughts, understanding the roots of these feelings is paramount. Embracing this awareness can guide us towards growth and self-improvement. A significant first step in this journey involves identifying triggers. Emotional triggers are those events, comments, or situations that spark an intense emotional reaction. These can vary greatly from person to person and may include scenarios like rejection, betrayal, or criticism (Raypole, 2020).

By recognizing these triggers, one can begin to understand why certain situations lead to feelings of inadequacy. For instance, a critical comment from a colleague might remind you of a past event where your efforts went unacknowledged. This recollection can evoke emotions linked to not feeling good enough, which is a common insecurity. Understanding this association helps demystify the origin of these feelings, allowing for more informed responses rather than reactive emotions.

Once aware of these triggers, it becomes crucial to document them through a practice like journaling. By consistently jotting down thoughts and feelings related to one's insecurities, patterns begin to emerge. Journaling allows individuals to track the instances that provoke these emotions, notice their frequency, and observe any recurring themes over time. Through this structured observation, the abstract nature of insecurities becomes tangible and easier to manage. Writing also provides a safe space to express emotions without fear of judgment, thus acting as a therapeutic exercise promoting self-reflection and clarity.

Breaking down negative self-talk forms another essential strategy in confronting insecurities. Often, our internal dialogues are filled with irrational and harsh criticisms that hinder healing and growth. Analyzing these negative dialogues is key to shifting perceptions and fostering a healthier self-image. For example, if a thought arises such as "I'm not as capable as others," it's beneficial to challenge this notion by reflecting on personal accomplishments and abilities. Substituting self-deprecating comments with affirming truths nurtures self-worth and encourages resilience against negative thoughts.

Furthermore, realizing the shared nature of insecurities among women can offer reassurance and a sense of community. Many women experience similar challenges regarding self-esteem and confidence, often driven by societal pressures and comparisons. Understanding that these insecurities are not unique but part of a broader shared experience can be liberating. Recognizing this commonality fosters solidarity and collective strategies for overcoming insecurity, rather than facing it in isolation. Engaging in discussions about these shared experiences can lead to supportive networks where individuals uplift each other, promote healing, and share resources for personal development.

Incorporating these approaches requires conscious effort and dedication. To identify triggers effectively, individuals should maintain a heightened sense of self-awareness and mindfulness. Keeping a journal demands consistency and honesty with oneself to truly capture the essence of one's experiences and emotions. Rest assured that the process itself is enlightening, uncovering insights that pave the way for personal growth.

Additionally, breaking down negative self-talk involves persistence and courage to confront deeply ingrained beliefs about oneself. It requires a shift in narrative, transforming moments of self-doubt into opportunities for affirmation. Such transformation does not happen overnight; instead, it is a gradual process, akin to rewiring the mind to embrace positivity and self-compassion over critique.

Lastly, finding commonality in insecurities calls for openness and vulnerability. Sharing personal insecurities demands trust and the willingness to embrace vulnerability for the sake of communal strength. However, doing so creates boundless possibilities for growth and connection, reinforcing the idea that we are not alone in our struggles.

Mindfulness Techniques for Calming Negative Thoughts

Breathing deeply is one of the most accessible mindfulness techniques, allowing individuals to manage stress and anxiety effectively. By focusing on intentional breath, one can interrupt negative thought cycles that often accompany feelings of insecurity or self-doubt. The act of deep breathing lowers heart rate and induces a state of calmness, making it easier to refocus thoughts away from distressing patterns. Consider practicing deep breathing exercises by sitting comfortably and closing your eyes, visualizing each breath moving in and out like ocean waves. This visualization aids in breaking the cycle of negativity, transforming the breath into a tool for emotional regulation.

Mindful meditation goes beyond simple breath control to direct attention entirely toward the present moment. This form of meditation helps diminish the overwhelming impact of anxiety by fostering a conscious awareness of the here and now. It encourages practitioners to acknowledge their thoughts without judgment, reducing the power those thoughts hold over them. To practice mindful meditation, find a quiet space, sit comfortably, and focus on sensations in the body, such as warmth or pressure where the body contacts the ground. If distracting thoughts emerge, note them nonjudgmentally and gently bring attention back to the body. Regular practice enhances one's ability to remain grounded amid unsettling thoughts, promoting overall mental clarity and peace.

Visualization techniques are another powerful way to manage intrusive thoughts and build resilience. By creating vivid mental images of serene places or positive outcomes, individuals can distract themselves from negative thinking and cultivate inner strength. Visualization works by diverting attention from anxiety-inducing thoughts, replacing them with tranquil imagery that calms the mind and body. Try picturing yourself in a soothing environment—a beach at sunrise, a quiet forest, or a cozy room—whenever anxious thoughts arise. Picture every detail vividly: the sounds, scents, colors, and temperatures. This immersive approach helps transport the mind to safety and security, providing respite from distress.

Gratitude practices are also essential tools in shifting focus from insecurities toward appreciation of life's positive aspects. Integrating gratitude into daily routines can significantly alter perspective, leading to improved emotional well-being. Cultivating gratitude involves recognizing simple joys and achievements, which offsets the tendency to dwell on perceived inadequacies. Start by dedicating a few moments each day to reflect on things you're thankful for, no matter how small. Write them down, or speak them softly to yourself, letting gratitude fill your mind with warmth and contentment. Over time, this practice trains your brain to notice and value the positives amidst life's challenges, thus reinforcing resilient and optimistic habits.

To integrate these techniques effectively, it's important to establish a consistent mindfulness routine. Regular practice not only alleviates immediate anxiety but also builds long-term resilience against stress. Begin by dedicating just a few minutes each day to one or more of these techniques. As comfort with the practice grows, gradually increase the duration or complexity. For example, start with simple breathing exercises, and as proficiency develops, incorporate visualization or gratitude reflections. Consistency nurtures familiarity and makes mindfulness second nature, offering tranquility even during the most turbulent times.

Each technique complements the others, forming a holistic approach to confronting insecurities and negative thoughts. Deep breathing provides a foundation for calming the physiological response to stress, while mindful meditation and visualization techniques help restructure habitual patterns of thought. Combining these with gratitude practices shifts attention from what's lacking to what's present, enriching life with positivity. Together, they empower individuals to take control of their mental landscape, transforming challenges into opportunities for growth and self-discovery.

While these techniques are universally beneficial, they can be particularly impactful for women navigating personal growth alongside demanding roles, individuals healing from trauma, and mentors guiding others through similar journeys. Breathing deeply and meditating mindfully pave avenues for healing and empowerment, fostering self-esteem and confidence. Visualizations reinforce one's mental fortitude, preparing them to handle life's unpredictability with grace. Gratitude, meanwhile, reinforces self-worth and unity, reminding us of shared experiences and collective progress.

Reframing Failures as Learning Experiences

Part of personal growth involves transforming how we perceive failures. Rather than viewing them as final judgments of our abilities or self-worth, they should be seen as stepping stones toward improvement and resilience. By embracing a growth mindset, individuals realize that their capabilities can evolve through dedication and hard work. This perspective allows us to approach challenges not as insurmountable obstacles, but as opportunities for refining our skills and understanding.

Cultivating a growth mindset begins with recognizing that every skill and ability can be developed over time. As Carol Dweck points out, the belief that intelligence and talent are fixed traits limits growth. When you believe that your potential can expand with effort, you become more open to tackling difficulties head-on. In this way, challenges become less intimidating—they're simply parts of the journey to mastery. Reflecting on figures like Thomas Edison, whose numerous failures led to eventual success, reinforces the idea that perseverance coupled with incremental learning leads to breakthrough achievements.

However, merely adopting a growth mindset is not enough. It is crucial to actively analyze past experiences and reflect on what didn't work and why. This analysis helps extract valuable lessons that inform future decisions, preventing similar mistakes and reducing feelings of shame associated with failure. By understanding that everyone encounters setbacks, we can shift our focus from the negative impact of failure towards its educational value.

When reflecting on past experiences, ask yourself: What specific actions led to the outcome? What could have been done differently? And most importantly, what has this taught me about my strengths and areas for development? Journaling these reflections can provide clarity and serve as a reference for future endeavors.

Celebrating efforts regardless of outcomes is another essential practice. It's vital to recognize and affirm the hard work you've invested in a process, even if it doesn't lead to immediate success. Acknowledging every small victory builds confidence and fosters a sense of self-worth that isn't solely tied to successful outcomes. For example, completing a challenging project or presentation is an achievement in itself, irrespective of the reception it receives. Such acknowledgment encourages persistence and resilience, nurturing an internal sense of accomplishment.

Furthermore, engaging in regular activities that highlight effort, such as setting small, achievable goals and rewarding yourself upon completion, can reinforce this habit. Progress becomes more visible, and motivation grows when the focus is on consistent effort rather than instant triumphs. Recognizing that effort is a sign of progress keeps the momentum alive and reduces the fear of failing, knowing that each attempt is just another step forward.

Sharing stories of failure with others is equally powerful. When we openly discuss our setbacks and how we've overcome them, we create a space where vulnerability is appreciated rather than shamed. This sharing not only provides relief and connection for the storyteller but also offers valuable insights and encouragement to listeners facing similar challenges. The camaraderie built through shared experiences proves that no one is alone in their struggles and that mutual support can empower collective growth.

Such dialogues can take place in various settings—whether among friends, support groups, or professional circles—and foster an environment where learning from mistakes is valued. Hearing how someone managed to pick themselves up after a challenging period can inspire others to persist with their own journeys. Encouraging discussions around failure also demystifies the concept and normalizes the ups and downs of personal and professional paths.

Using Affirmations to Nurture Positivity

In the journey of confronting our insecurities and negative thoughts, affirmations provide a powerful means to cultivate self-love and encourage positive thinking. By nurturing this practice, individuals can transform their perspectives, turning self-doubt into empowerment.

Creating Personalized Affirmations is a profound step towards self-discovery and healing. These tailored affirmations resonate deeply on an individual level, addressing specific insecurities and life circumstances. For instance, if someone struggles with body image, an affirmation like "I appreciate my body for all it does for me" can gradually shift the narrative from criticism to gratitude. The key here is personal resonance; the affirmations must align with core values and genuine aspirations. This personalization ensures that each affirmation carries meaningful weight, acting as a counterbalance to negative self-talk.

Integrating Daily Affirmation Practices into one's routine is essential for reinforcing self-acceptance and rewiring negative thought patterns. Start by choosing a moment in your day—perhaps morning or night—to quietly repeat your affirmations. Consistency is crucial; much like physical exercise, the mental muscles need regular workouts to grow stronger. This practice may initially feel awkward or forced, but with time, it fosters a fresh pathway in the brain, gradually replacing doubt with confidence. Engaging in these practices continuously helps solidify the habit, making positivity a natural reflex rather than a forced decision. (LCSW, 2023)

A practical way to enhance the impact of affirmations is through Recording and Reviewing them. Writing affirmations in a journal or recording them on an audio device offers a tangible reminder of commitment to personal growth. It allows individuals to revisit these positive statements anytime reinforcement is needed. Reading past entries can offer comfort during difficult times, serving as proof of emotional progress and resilience. Additionally, reviewing these affirmations can help refine them over time, ensuring they evolve alongside personal development and continue to address current needs effectively. Documenting thoughts not only strengthens the message but also provides a sense of accomplishment and assurance that gradual changes are happening.

Affirmations in Challenging Times act as anchors, grounding individuals when instability threatens to take hold. During moments of struggle—whether facing rejection, failure, or emotional upheaval—affirmations such as "I am enough just as I am" reaffirm inherent worth and bolster resilience. These reminders help maintain perspective, offering stability amidst chaos. Drawing strength from such affirmations encourages the belief that challenges can be overcome, fostering a mindset resilient against adversity. When repeated during difficult moments, these words become more than just statements— they become lifelines that support healing and perseverance.

While affirmations are transformative tools, it's important to approach them with patience and realism. They are not instant fixes for deep-seated issues but should be viewed as part of a broader toolkit for managing emotions healthily. Especially for those grappling with significant mental health concerns, professional guidance remains crucial alongside affirmation practices. However, keeping expectations balanced allows affirmations to work effectively within their scope, eventually leading to noticeable shifts in mindset over time.

The benefits of incorporating affirmations into daily life extend beyond immediate emotional relief. Research has shown that self-love affirmations increase self-compassion, helping individuals treat themselves with kindness and understanding (Gupta, 2024). By challenging negative self-talk, affirmations contribute to improved self-esteem and promote positive thinking, gradually replacing pessimistic beliefs with healthier thoughts and behaviors. Emotional wellbeing naturally follows these changes, as feelings of happiness, gratitude, and inner peace become more frequent companions.

To maximize the impact of affirmations, consider integrating them creatively into various aspects of life. For example, placing written affirmations on mirrors or workspaces serves as constant visual encouragement throughout the day. Setting phone reminders to read affirmations periodically infuses positivity into routine activities. Similarly, using affirmations as motivation during workouts can drive physical resilience as well as mental resolve. Maintaining a gratitude journal also pairs well with affirmations, encouraging reflection on both intrinsic and extrinsic blessings as part of a holistic approach to positivity.

Sharing affirmations with friends or family members invites collective energy into the practice, creating a supportive network that bolsters mutual growth. By exchanging encouraging words, individuals build environments rich in positivity, promoting shared success and joy. This collective aspect reminds us of the interconnected nature of human experience, where individual efforts contribute to a greater tapestry of love and acceptance.

Managing Comparison and Jealousy in a Healthy Way

In a world where comparisons have become second nature, recognizing the triggers that lead us down this perilous path is crucial. We often find ourselves trapped in a cycle, unaware of the subtle cues that propel us into envy and dissatisfaction. By identifying these triggers, we empower ourselves to manage our emotions proactively. This journey begins with self-awareness. Consider social media, for example—a virtual playground where snippets of other people's curated lives are displayed like trophies. The seemingly perfect vacation photos or professional achievements can ignite feelings of inadequacy. Becoming conscious of how these encounters make you feel allows you to navigate your emotional responses more effectively. Keep a journal to note contexts or scenarios that spark comparisons; over time, patterns will emerge, offering insights into moments when you should exercise caution.

Alongside identifying triggers, limiting social media consumption becomes a vital strategy. The narratives we encounter online are often a refined version of reality, making us question the authenticity of our own experiences. Studies have shown that reducing exposure to these curated narratives can lessen the occurrence of negative comparisons and the subsequent emotional toll they take (jaceylenae, 2020). It's about creating boundaries—deciding on specific times of day to engage with social media or even taking periodic breaks to recalibrate your mindset. Such practices can help redirect focus towards real-life interactions and personal growth rather than endless scrolling sessions.

Moving forward, cultivating compassion towards others plays an integral role in transforming jealousy into admiration. When we encounter someone who seems to embody traits or achievements we desire, instead of succumbing to envy, we can choose empathy. Recognize their journey and the effort behind their accomplishments. Celebrate their success as if it were your own. Acknowledging the hard work and dedication of others fosters positive connections and diminishes the bitterness associated with jealousy. Moreover, practicing compassion invites a sense of community, reminding us that supporting one another enhances collective well-being.

Reflecting on your personal journey can further counteract

negative comparisons. Each person's path is uniquely theirs, marked by triumphs and challenges alike. Focusing on individual progress rather than measuring against external benchmarks emphasizes growth and self-improvement. Regularly assess your accomplishments, big or small, and celebrate them. Remind yourself of past obstacles you've overcome and lessons learned along the way. This practice not only nurtures gratitude but also reinforces confidence in your abilities.

The new perspectives gained from understanding comparison triggers, managing social media usage, cultivating compassion, and reflecting on personal journeys contribute to a healthier mindset. It's important to remain committed to these strategies, even as life offers fresh challenges. Developing these habits requires discipline and patience, but the rewards are immense—granting peace and clarity in an otherwise tumultuous world. Remember that everyone fights unseen battles, concealed beneath polished exteriors, so approach each encounter with kindness—for yourself and others.

Final Thoughts

In this chapter, we've explored the various ways insecurities and negative thoughts can hinder our personal growth and how recognizing these patterns is essential for transformation. We've discussed how understanding triggers can provide insight into why certain situations provoke feelings of inadequacy. By embracing practices such as journaling, individuals can document and track emotional responses, gaining clarity and control over these experiences. Furthermore, breaking down negative self-talk allows one to challenge internal criticisms, promoting a healthier self-image. This journey of self-discovery and reflection highlights the shared nature of insecurities, encouraging support and connection among women who face similar challenges.

Building on this foundation, mindfulness techniques like deep breathing, meditation, and gratitude practices offer powerful tools to calm and redirect negative thought patterns. Integrating these methods into daily lives fosters resilience and enhances mental well-being. Additionally, reframing failures as learning opportunities enables personal growth and perseverance, while affirmations nurture positivity and self-worth. By managing comparisons and jealousy through self-awareness and compassion, individuals can move towards appreciating their unique paths. Collectively, these strategies empower women, individuals healing from trauma, and mentors guiding others to approach life with renewed confidence and strength, transforming insecurities into stepping stones for empowerment and development.

The Art of Self-Compassion and Emotional Healing

Self-compassion and emotional healing are deeply intertwined, forming the cornerstone of a life filled with resilience and recovery. Understanding how to cultivate self-compassion is essential in managing emotional challenges and fostering a mindset that thrives on kindness and understanding. The journey toward emotional healing involves acknowledging one's own pain and responding with empathy, which can prevent the cycle of negativity from festering into deeper emotional scars. It's about learning to navigate through emotional turmoil with gentleness and an open heart, allowing for a profound transformation that aligns with personal growth and strength. Such compassion not only aids in recovering from emotional wounds but also builds a foundation for enduring happiness and inner peace.

This chapter delves into various strategies aimed at nurturing a compassionate mindset that underpins emotional recovery. It explores practical approaches like self-forgiveness, encouraging readers to address their imperfections without self-judgment. Readers will also find discussions on cultivating gratitude as a means to foster self-love reinforce the idea that appreciating life's positives can significantly enhance emotional well-being. By examining these aspects, the chapter provides a comprehensive guide to embracing imperfection as a part of individuality, offering tools and insights to empower readers in their journey of self-discovery and healing. Additionally, the chapter unravels the significance of creating personal mantras and mindfulness practices, emphasizing their role in developing emotional resilience and enhancing mental clarity. Through these narratives, individuals are equipped with the ability to transform their relationship with themselves, paving the way for enriched emotional vitality and authentic living.

Practicing Forgiveness Towards Oneself and Others

Forgiveness is a powerful tool for emotional healing, offering individuals the chance to release themselves from the burdens of resentment and guilt. At its core, forgiveness is about letting go—letting go of the negative emotions and thoughts that tie us to past grievances. When individuals choose to forgive, they open the door to a life unshackled by the weight of anger and bitterness. It's essential to understand that forgiveness doesn't necessarily mean forgetting or condoning the actions of those who have hurt us. Instead, it involves freeing oneself from the destructive hold these feelings can have on our emotional well-being.

Prolonged harbouring of grudges can lead to significant emotional distress. Imagine carrying a heavy load everywhere you go—it's exhausting and unsustainable. In a similar fashion, holding onto past grievances drains mental energy and impedes personal joy. Research consistently highlights the link between chronic resentment and adverse mental health outcomes like anxiety and depression (Johns Hopkins Medicine, 2019). Letting go of these longstanding resentments paves the way for emotional lightness and increased happiness. The decision to forgive can clear away the clouds of negativity, allowing positive emotions to flourish.

Self-forgiveness is another critical aspect of this journey. It begins with acknowledging one's wrongdoings, a step that requires humility and courage. Facing our mistakes head-on, rather than sweeping them under the rug, helps lay the foundation for genuine healing. By owning up to past actions and understanding their impact, individuals start to dismantle the walls built from self-blame and shame. This acknowledgment is not about wallowing in guilt but about accepting responsibility as a means to move forward positively. The practice of self-forgiveness can transform guilt into learning experiences, fostering an environment conducive to personal growth and acceptance.

Offering forgiveness, whether to others or oneself, significantly boosts mental health and fosters resilience. The act of forgiving cultivates psychological freedom, reducing the stress associated with lingering animosities. Forgiveness has been shown to improve overall well-being and even physical health by lowering blood pressure and decreasing levels of anxiety, depression, and stress (Johns Hopkins Medicine, 2019). Embracing forgiveness invites peace of mind and emotional stability, empowering individuals to cope better with life's challenges.

The health benefits of forgiveness extend beyond mental wellness. Studies have indicated that forgiving people enjoy better sleep, improved immune function, and lower risks of heart-related issues (*Key Insights into the Psychology of Forgiveness | Resiliency</i>, 2024). The physiological effects are noticeable: anger and resentment can trigger the body's fight-or-flight response, increasing heart rate and blood pressure. On the other hand, forgiveness calms these responses, promoting relaxation and recovery from emotional upheaval.

Forgiveness also plays a vital role in relationships. It mends broken bonds by fostering understanding and empathy between individuals. The decision to forgive reaches beyond the personal to affect interpersonal dynamics, as it encourages healthier interactions and strengthens connections. Trust and communication benefit from forgiving environments, facilitating open dialogue and mutual respect. Individuals and communities thrive on such foundations, where forgiveness acts as a cornerstone of empathy and unity.

It's crucial to distinguish between forgiveness and reconciliation. Forgiving someone does not obligate you to maintain a relationship with them or restore trust immediately. Forgiveness is primarily for the forgiver—it is an internal process aimed at releasing emotional baggage. While reconciliation might be a natural outcome in some cases, it's not a prerequisite for forgiveness.

Mindful techniques can support the process of forgiveness, providing individuals with tools to navigate this path with more ease and clarity. Practices like meditation and mindfulness encourage present-focused awareness and non-judgmental acceptance of thoughts and emotions. These practices foster greater self-awareness and emotional regulation, which are pivotal for extending forgiveness. Techniques such as loving-kindness meditation, which focuses on cultivating compassion, can make the act of forgiving feel more accessible and genuine.

Radical acceptance, a mindful approach that complements

forgiveness, involves embracing reality without fighting against it. Through radical acceptance, individuals acknowledge the pain and injustice they have experienced without becoming consumed by anger and resistance. This approach encourages a shift in perspective, enabling people to forgive by focusing on personal healing rather than dwelling on the past.

One common hurdle to forgiveness is the fear of letting offenders off the hook. It's important to emphasize that forgiveness doesn't absolve others of responsibility or negate justice. Rather, it's about taking back control over one's emotional state and refusing to be shackled by someone else's actions. In forgiving, individuals reclaim their power and autonomy, choosing to prioritize their peace over prolonged suffering.

Navigating Through Emotional Pain with Kindness

In the journey of emotional healing and developing a compassionate mindset, approaching one's own emotional pain with kindness is fundamental. The process begins with recognizing and acknowledging emotional pain, a crucial first step toward recovery. Acknowledgement allows individuals to validate their feelings rather than dismiss them, providing the necessary space for healing. It's important to understand that emotional pain, much like physical pain, signals an area that needs attention and care. Recognizing this can often be difficult due to societal pressures to remain strong or unaffected by adversity; however, ignoring emotional distress only prolongs suffering.

Once emotional pain is acknowledged, treating oneself with compassion becomes pivotal in promoting alleviation. Self-compassion involves offering oneself the same understanding and support one would offer a friend. This approach lessens negative self-talk, which is a common hindrance to emotional wellness. When faced with emotional challenges, reframing thoughts from self-criticism to self-kindness can shift perspectives and reduce symptoms of anxiety and depression. For instance, instead of berating oneself for feeling sad or distressed, try expressing empathy and allowing yourself to experience these emotions without judgment. This mental shift not only mitigates harsh self-judgment but also nurtures emotional resilience.

Engaging in nurturing self-talk during tough times plays a significant role in aiding recovery. Positive affirmations and compassionate dialogue towards oneself help maintain a balanced state of mind. During moments of emotional turmoil, reminding yourself of personal strengths and past successes can reinforce self-worth and provide comfort. It's helpful to practice self-compassionate phrases such as, "I'm doing my best given the circumstances," which can ease the burden of perfectionism and encourage a more forgiving attitude toward personal struggles.

Furthermore, seeking support from friends or professionals fosters a sense of connectedness that is vital for emotional recovery. Sharing experiences with loved ones not only alleviates feelings of isolation but also opens avenues for receiving guidance and emotional support. Often, simply knowing someone is willing to listen provides significant comfort and reassurance. Social connections act as a buffer against stress, creating a support network that enhances mental well-being. In cases where reaching out to friends or family isn't feasible, professional help can provide structured support through therapy or counselling. Mental health professionals are equipped with tools and strategies tailored to support individual recovery journeys, helping people navigate complex emotions and fostering a deeper understanding of self-compassion.

In addition to external support, incorporating practices such as mindfulness and meditation into daily routines can aid in maintaining emotional balance. Mindfulness encourages present-moment awareness and acceptance of emotions without judgment, allowing individuals to observe their thoughts and feelings without becoming overwhelmed by them. This practice cultivates a gentle and compassionate stance toward oneself, reinforcing the principles of self-compassion in everyday life.

On a practical level, nurturing oneself through physical self-care can also play a role in managing emotional pain. Ensuring adequate rest, nutrition, and engaging in activities that bring joy contribute to overall well-being. These activities serve as reminders of self-worth and are acts of self-love, reinforcing the importance of being kind to oneself. Engaging in hobbies or creative pursuits can provide an outlet for expression and reflection, offering solace and meaning even in challenging times.

Lastly, it's essential to remember that overcoming emotional pain is not an overnight process. Patience and persistence are required as healing unfolds gradually. Each step taken toward self-kindness and compassion contributes to building emotional resilience, equipping individuals with the strength needed to face future adversities more effectively. By embracing self-compassion, individuals can transform their relationship with themselves, paving the way for a fulfilling and emotionally enriched life.

The Role of Gratitude in Fostering Self-Love

Gratitude is a potent tool in nurturing self-love and acceptance, transforming our focus from life's negatives to its many positives. It acts as a gentle reminder that there is always something worth appreciating, even amid adversity. This shift in focus plays a crucial role in fostering positive emotions, which are foundational for emotional healing and resilience.

When we cultivate gratitude, we actively redirect our awareness away from deficiencies and towards the abundance of small blessings in our daily lives. This practice can significantly reduce stress levels and enhance our overall emotional state. Gratitude allows us to break free from cycles of negativity, encouraging us to develop a more optimistic outlook on life. This change in perspective is not merely about ignoring problems but rather acknowledging the whole picture, including the good aspects that often go unnoticed.

One effective way to embed gratitude into our lives is through daily practices such as keeping a gratitude journal or creating a gratitude jar. The act of writing down things we are thankful for—no matter how big or small—helps solidify the importance of these positive elements in our minds. Over time, this ritual reinforces our ability to recognize and recall them, even when circumstances are challenging. It is in these quiet moments of reflection that we begin to appreciate the abundance we have, leading to greater self-compassion.

Daily gratitude practices serve as reminders of what truly matters, helping us remember our values and priorities. By focusing on gratitude, individuals develop a deeper understanding of themselves and their needs, which promotes personal growth and emotional maturity. Through this process, people often find that their insecurities diminish, replaced by a stronger sense of self-worth and acceptance.

Sharing gratitude with others extends its benefits beyond ourselves, reaching into our relationships and social connections. When we express appreciation to those around us, it enhances mutual respect and understanding, forming a foundation for stronger, more supportive relationships. Expressing gratitude also acts as a bridge during times of conflict, providing a pathway back to connectivity and empathy. By fostering positive interactions, gratitude supports an environment where both parties feel valued and understood, contributing to overall well-being.

The impact of gratitude extends well into the future, as long-term gratitude practices significantly reshape our perspectives and contribute to sustained happiness. By consistently practicing gratitude, individuals develop a habit of recognizing the good, which cultivates an enduring sense of contentment. This enhanced perspective gradually becomes a natural part of everyday thinking, leading to improved mood and increased resilience against life's inevitable setbacks.

Gratitude not only boosts individual happiness but also serves as an anchor during difficult times. Its effects on mental health are profound; studies have shown that gratitude can alleviate symptoms of depression and anxiety, offering solace and hope to those who practice it regularly (Chowdhury, 2019). Additionally, the physical benefits of gratitude are well-documented, with research indicating improvements in sleep quality, reduced blood pressure, and decreased levels of chronic pain.

In order to fully harness the power of gratitude, it may be helpful to incorporate guidelines for building a solid gratitude practice. Start by setting aside a few minutes each day to reflect on three things you are grateful for. These could be as simple as a warm cup of tea, a kind word from a friend, or the beauty of a sunset. Consistency is key; maintaining this practice over time will strengthen your ability to notice and value the positive aspects of your life.

As you progress, consider sharing your gratitude with others through simple gestures, such as writing thank-you notes or verbally expressing appreciation. Engage in conversations where gratitude is centred, allowing it to flow naturally and authentically. Remember, gratitude is a skill that can be cultivated and enriched by regular practice and reflection.

Creating a Personal Mantra for Healing

In the journey toward emotional healing and self-compassion, personal mantras can be powerful tools. These affirmations not only promote resilience but also help cultivate a more positive mindset. By regularly incorporating personal mantras into our daily routine, we can transform how we approach life's challenges.

To begin with, understanding the role of mantras as affirmations is crucial. Mantras are simple, positive phrases that are repeated to reinforce a belief or intention. They serve as a mental anchor, providing stability during uncertain or distressing times. The repetitive nature of mantras helps them become ingrained in our minds, much like learning lyrics to a song through repetition. This ongoing practice fosters a resilient outlook by counteracting negative thoughts with positivity and strength.

Creating a personalized mantra begins with identifying

keywords or phrases that resonate with the individual. These should reflect hope and healing, tailored to the specific challenges or goals one faces. For instance, someone recovering from trauma might choose words like "strength," "peace," or "heal." Personalizing the mantra ensures it remains meaningful and directly connected to one's emotional needs. This personalization makes it more impactful, offering a sense of ownership and empowerment over one's emotional journey.

Using mantras during periods of stress is especially beneficial in reframing negative thought patterns. Stress often triggers an automatic response to negative thinking, which can exacerbate feelings of anxiety or hopelessness. By consciously shifting focus to a mantra, individuals can interrupt this cycle. For example, repeating a phrase like "I am calm, I am strong" during a stressful moment can redirect thoughts, helping to alleviate immediate tension.

Consistent use of mantras is key to integrating mindfulness into everyday life. Mindfulness, the practice of staying present and focused on the current moment, can significantly enhance emotional well-being. Mantras contribute to this by anchoring attention and reducing distractions. As the mantra becomes a habitual part of daily routines, it naturally promotes a state of mindfulness. Whether used in morning routines, while commuting, or during quiet reflection, these affirmations can seamlessly blend into life's fabric, offering a steady source of comfort and clarity.

The broader impact of adopting personal mantras is supported by emerging research. Studies have shown that practices such as mantra meditation can positively influence mood and cognitive function. According to a systematic review by Lynch et al., mantra-based meditation may benefit mental health outcomes like anxiety, stress, depression, and psychological distress (Mantra: A Powerful Way to Improve Your Well-Being, 2019). Additionally, evidence suggests that mantras can enhance brain activity related to sensory perception and memory function, further highlighting their potential for improving emotional resilience.

Moreover, the integration of mantras into daily practices supports the development of a more constructive internal dialogue. It is widely acknowledged that our thoughts and language can greatly impact self-esteem and mood. Positive affirmations reinforced through mantras challenge detrimental self-talk and foster a nurturing and compassionate internal environment. Embracing this shift leads to increased self-confidence and a more balanced emotional state, which are essential components for building long-term resilience.

For those seeking guidance on how to effectively incorporate personal mantras, it is helpful to start small. Begin with a few simple phrases aligned with your current emotional needs. Practice saying these aloud each day, perhaps setting aside five minutes in the morning or evening for focused repetition. Over time, expand the practice to include moments of stress or uncertainty, allowing the mantra to guide you back to a place of calm focus. Observe how these words alter both your internal dialogue and external reactions, gradually transforming negative perspectives into opportunities for growth.

Embracing Imperfections as Part of Individuality

In the journey of self-discovery and emotional healing, embracing our imperfections can play a pivotal role. Often, societal pressures push us towards perfectionism, leading to chronic dissatisfaction. Perfectionism is not merely striving for excellence; it becomes detrimental when it imposes an unattainable standard that we constantly fail to meet. This constant chase for flawlessness creates a persistent sense of inadequacy, overshadowing our achievements and authentic selves. It's essential to acknowledge that while the pursuit of betterment can be positive, the relentless demand for perfection is unrealistic and damaging.

Recognizing that nobody is without flaws allows us to see our imperfections not as liabilities but as integral components of our unique identity. Each person's life story is a tapestry of diverse experiences, and these imperfections shape who we are, giving depth and richness to our narratives. By celebrating what makes us different, we can break free from the confines of comparison and appreciate the individual journeys that contribute to our collective human experience. Every imperfection holds a lesson or a strength that enriches our lives and those around us.

To foster acceptance of our imperfections, engaging in practical exercises can be incredibly beneficial. One such exercise is journaling. By writing about our perceived imperfections without judgment, we can explore their origins and impacts on our lives. This practice encourages introspection and helps us identify patterns, fostering greater self-awareness. Additionally, surrounding ourselves with affirmations that focus on self-love and acceptance can gradually transform our internal dialogue.

Another effective exercise involves seeking out small daily triumphs that emphasize personal strengths over weaknesses. Reflecting on moments when our imperfections led to unexpected positive outcomes can shift our perception, highlighting beauty beyond perceived flaws. For example, someone might find that their tendency to overthink leads to thoroughness and attention to detail in their work. Recognizing how these quirks manifest positively can help us appreciate them as strengths rather than drawbacks.

Embracing self-acceptance ultimately fosters higher self-esteem and reduces anxiety. When we stop trying to mould ourselves into external standards and start valuing our inherent qualities, we develop a more grounded sense of self-worth. This shift can diminish the anxiety associated with striving for perfection and the fear of failure. By aligning our self-image with reality rather than an idealized version, we free ourselves from the burden of perpetual dissatisfaction.

Moreover, self-acceptance enhances our relationships. When we are comfortable with who we are, we tend to project authenticity, attracting genuine connections with others. People often resonate with those who embrace their imperfections because it allows for vulnerability and relatability. In contrast to the polished facades many present, showing our true selves invites deeper understanding and empathy, paving the way for meaningful interactions.

For individuals who have faced past trauma, accepting imperfections can be particularly liberating. Trauma often leaves individuals with feelings of shame or brokenness. By reframing imperfections as the scars of survival and growth, they become symbols of resilience rather than deficits. This perspective empowers individuals to redefine their narrative, focusing on strength and recovery rather than victimhood.

Educators and counsellors can play a significant role in guiding others toward this mindset. Encouraging an environment where uniqueness is celebrated rather than criticized sets a precedent for self-acceptance. By modelling this behaviour and promoting discussions about the value of diversity in personal traits and backgrounds, mentors can influence how others perceive themselves. Sharing stories of successful individuals who have embraced their flaws can also serve as powerful testimonials, inspiring those on similar journeys.

Furthermore, incorporating mindfulness practices such as meditation or deep-breathing exercises can support a compassionate approach towards oneself. These practices cultivate an awareness of the present moment, allowing individuals to observe their thoughts without immediate judgment. Over time, this nurtures a kinder internal voice, which is crucial for developing self-compassion and reducing negative self-talk.

Acceptance of imperfections, however, does not imply complacency. It does not mean ceasing personal growth or improvement. Rather, it provides a foundation of self-love from which we can pursue progress without the destructive backdrop of perfectionism. When we accept ourselves wholly, flaws included, we engage in personal development from a place of abundance rather than deficiency.

Concluding Thoughts

In navigating the depths of forgiveness and self-compassion, this chapter has illuminated the powerful role these practices play in emotional healing and building resilience. Recognizing that forgiveness is a deeply personal journey allows individuals to release burdens of resentment and guilt. This process fosters psychological freedom, enabling both mental and physical health benefits. By offering forgiveness to oneself and others, a renewed sense of peace and stability can emerge, enhancing relationships through empathy and understanding. Moreover, the willingness to forgive supports the cultivation of a compassionate mindset, which can significantly mitigate the impacts of anxiety, depression, and stress, ultimately strengthening one's emotional fortitude.

Equally crucial is the practice of engaging with one's emotional pain using kindness and self-compassion. Acknowledging emotional distress as a signal for care rather than weakness opens pathways for authentic healing. Through self-compassionate techniques like positive affirmations and mindfulness practices, individuals can shift from self-criticism to supportive inner dialogue. These shifts promote emotional resilience and pave the way toward overcoming past trauma with patience and persistence. Additionally, embracing imperfections as part of individuality liberates individuals from the exhausting pursuit of perfectionism. This acceptance, underpinned by gratitude, redefines personal narratives into stories of strength and growth, empowering women to face future challenges with confidence.

Empowering Your Unique Journey: Transformative Tools

Utilizing transformative tools and narratives can profoundly impact personal development, particularly for women navigating their unique life journeys. These methods are not merely about change but about empowerment—providing practical strategies to embrace one's individuality through various self-help techniques. The journey begins with recognizing the power in these tools, which hold the potential to reshape our perspectives and propel us toward goals that align with our deepest desires. By engaging with these resources, individuals can harness a sense of agency and purpose, transforming challenges into opportunities for growth.

In this chapter, readers will delve into the specifics of crafting a vision board, exploring its potential as a tool for aspiration setting. The process and benefits of this visual representation are outlined, offering insights into how such an exercise can ground dreams in reality. Additionally, the chapter introduces journaling as a reflective practice to clarify thoughts and emotions, fostering self-awareness and emotional resilience. Further exploration will include structured goal-setting techniques to provide clear pathways toward achieving personal milestones. Finally, creative expression and meditation practices are presented as avenues for emotional exploration and inner peace, reinforcing the transformative journey. This comprehensive approach equips readers with actionable strategies to navigate their paths with confidence and intention.

Crafting a Vision Board for Aspiration Setting

Visualizing goals and aspirations can be a powerful tool in one's personal development journey. By creating a tangible representation of our dreams, we give them life and presence, allowing them to become a more significant part of our daily consciousness. The first step in this process is to gather images and words that resonate deeply with personal goals. This could include anything from photographs and magazine cutouts to hand-drawn sketches or meaningful quotes. These elements should speak to your innermost desires, acting as a visual affirmation of what you hope to achieve. Once collected, they form the foundational pieces of your vision board.

In terms of materials, both digital and physical tools can be highly effective for crafting these vision boards. Digital platforms like Pinterest allow for curated collections of inspiration, while apps such as Milanote provide structured layouts and easy editing options. For those who prefer a hands-on approach, traditional poster boards or corkboards offer a tactile experience that can be just as fulfilling. Whether online or offline, these resources afford flexibility, enabling changes and additions as your aspirations evolve over time.

Next, it is essential to set specific intentions alongside the images on your vision board. This practice involves not only identifying what you want but also defining actionable steps to move toward those goals. For instance, if you have an image of a person running a marathon, note down the training plan and milestones required to complete one yourself. By doing so, you transform abstract wishes into concrete plans, empowering yourself to take control of your path.

Another critical aspect of maintaining the efficacy of a vision board is regular updates. Our dreams and circumstances change, and our visual representations should reflect that dynamism. Routinely revisiting and refreshing the vision board ensures it remains a true reflection of current aspirations, serving as an ongoing source of motivation. By replacing old images with new ones that capture your latest ambitions, you continuously align your focus with your evolving priorities. This process of constant renewal keeps the energy around your goals lively and engaging, spurring you on in your journey.

Creating a vision board is not merely an artistic endeavour; it's a profound exercise in self-discovery and clarity. As you lay out visuals and words, patterns may emerge that highlight recurring themes or values significant to you. These insights can further inform how you wish to direct your energies and efforts moving forward.

One guideline when setting up your vision board is to experiment with the layout to find what feels right for you. There is no single correct way to assemble a vision board, and the creative freedom involved can be incredibly liberating. You might choose to organize randomly for a free-flowing look or group related items to signify their relationship. Such arrangements can help underscore which aspects of your life you're focusing most on, providing additional insight into your priorities.

In considering the setup, color schemes can play a vital role.

Choosing complementary colours or even contrasting hues can enhance the visual appeal and make certain elements stand out. For example, brighter colours might symbolize passion or excitement, while softer tones could represent calm or peace. Incorporating textures and layers adds another dimension, making the board more tactile and interactive.

Once completed, place your vision board where you'll see it frequently. Whether hanging by your wardrobe mirror, above your workspace, or as a digital wallpaper, it should serve as a daily reminder of your commitments to yourself. This consistent exposure reinforces the importance of your goals and keeps them at the forefront of your mind.

The act of sharing your vision board with trusted friends or family members can also deepen its impact. Those close to you can offer encouragement and help hold you accountable, bolstering your determination to turn your visions into reality. However, remember that the primary purpose of the vision board is to guide and inspire you, so share selectively.

As life progresses, don't hesitate to start anew if necessary. Sometimes, starting from scratch allows for a clearer perspective and fresh energy towards new objectives. Just as seasons change, so too do personal circumstances and aspirations. Embrace these shifts as opportunities for growth and realignment.

Journaling as a Tool for Reflection and Clarity

Journaling is a powerful tool for self-reflection and personal growth, offering individuals a tangible means to explore their thoughts, emotions, and experiences. At its core, journaling serves as an intimate dialogue with oneself, where the act of writing becomes a journey toward greater self-understanding and healing.

For those new to journaling, exploring different techniques can provide varied pathways to insight. Gratitude journaling focuses on acknowledging and appreciating life's positives, fostering a mindset that attracts more positivity. By taking time to note things you are thankful for, even amid challenges, you cultivate gratitude, which has been linked to improved mental health and reduced stress (Sutton, 2018).

Stream-of-consciousness writing, on the other hand, allows the free flow of thoughts without the constraints of structure or grammar. This technique encourages a raw expression of emotions and ideas, promoting acceptance and understanding of your mental state. It's a liberating practice that aids in disentangling complex emotions and identifying underlying patterns in our thinking.

Consistency in journaling practices plays a crucial role in emotional processing and insight development. Like any meaningful habit, the benefits of journaling accrue over time. Writing regularly, whether daily or several times a week, helps individuals process emotions more effectively and develop a deeper understanding of recurring themes in their lives. For many, this consistent practice becomes a therapeutic outlet, reducing anxiety and facilitating cognitive defusion—creating distance between you and your thoughts (Tartakovsky, 2022).

To truly harness the potential of journaling, creating a supportive environment is essential. A quiet, comfortable space, free from distractions, fosters deep reflective writing. It's important to approach each session with openness and curiosity, allowing the mind to wander and explore. Some individuals find it helpful to begin with a meditation or relaxation exercise to clear their head before they start writing. This practice not only enhances focus but also primes the mind for introspection.

Furthermore, reviewing past journal entries serves as a valuable tool for recognizing progress and evolving perspectives. It provides a documented history of personal growth, capturing moments of joy, struggle, and transformation. By revisiting these entries, individuals can identify patterns, celebrate achievements, and gain insights into how their thoughts and feelings have shifted over time. Such reflection not only boosts motivation but also reinforces the resilience gained through overcoming previous challenges.

One effective way to maintain engagement in journaling is by setting specific intentions or prompts for each session. Prompts could range from exploring current emotions to reflecting on past experiences or contemplating future aspirations. These guided entries ensure that the writing remains focused and purposeful, directing attention to areas that need exploration. However, it's equally important to allow flexibility, letting the mind wander naturally if it veers off-topic, as this often leads to unexpected revelations.

Journaling, when approached with dedication and openness, serves as a mirror reflecting our inner world. It captures the nuances of emotional triggers, highlights shifts in values and beliefs, and provides clarity in confusing times. The page becomes a confidant, offering solace and understanding when verbal expression falls short. Women seeking empowerment through self-awareness will discover that journaling not only enhances self-esteem but also builds emotional resilience—a vital asset in navigating life's complexities.

Educators, mentors, and counsellors working with women may recommend journaling as a transformative practice. By encouraging clients or students to regularly record their thoughts and feelings, professionals can support individuals in developing coping strategies and fostering emotional intelligence. Journaling also acts as an adjunct tool in therapy, facilitating communication and deepening the client's understanding of their own experiences.

Engaging in Goal-Setting with Actionable Steps

Structured goal-setting can be a transformative tool for personal development. By boosting confidence and providing a sense of purpose, this method empowers individuals to navigate their unique journeys with clarity and intention. At the heart of effective goal-setting is the SMART criteria, which stands for Specific, Measurable, Achievable, Relevant, and Time-bound goals. This framework ensures that each goal is clear and actionable, providing a solid foundation on which to build.

Specificity in goal-setting involves clearly defining what you want to achieve. For example, rather than setting a vague goal like "get fit," a more specific goal would be "exercise three times a week for 30 minutes." Measurability allows you to track progress, providing motivation and a way to evaluate your efforts. Using concrete numbers or milestones, such as aiming to lose five pounds in a month, makes your progress tangible and motivates continued effort. Achievability ensures your goals are realistic, preventing discouragement from unachievable ambitions. Relevance aligns goals with broader life objectives or values, making them meaningful and motivating. Lastly, time-bound goals create urgency by setting deadlines and encouraging consistent action.

Once your goals are established using the SMART framework, breaking them into manageable steps is crucial to avoid overwhelm. Long-term goals, though essential, can often feel daunting. By dividing them into smaller tasks or milestones, you create a roadmap that makes the journey toward your larger objectives more accessible. For instance, if your long-term goal is to write a book, start by setting a goal to complete a chapter a month. This approach not only simplifies the process but also provides frequent opportunities for accomplishment, keeping motivation high.

Regular tracking and adjustment of goals are vital in reflecting personal growth and adapting to changing circumstances. Life is dynamic, and so should be your goals. Regularly reviewing your progress helps identify areas that require more focus or modification. Tools like journals or digital apps can assist in tracking achievements and setbacks, allowing for real-time insights into what strategies are working and what might need adjusting. This practice reinforces commitment and flexibility, ensuring that goals remain relevant and achievable as you evolve.

Collaborating with accountability partners adds another layer of support and motivation. Sharing your goals with someone who understands your aspirations fosters a supportive environment where encouragement and constructive feedback thrive. Accountability partners provide external motivation and help maintain focus, especially during challenging times. These relationships offer fresh perspectives, helping to overcome obstacles you may not have anticipated alone (Sudarshan Somanathan, 2024). Finding the right accountability partner requires identifying someone who shares similar values or has complementary goals, ensuring alignment and mutual support.

Creating a supportive environment for your goals involves

surrounding yourself with resources and people that encourage your journey. Whether it's joining a community group, attending workshops, or engaging in online forums, these networks can provide inspiration, guidance, and a sense of belonging. Revisiting past entries or experiences allows you to recognize patterns, celebrate growth, and adjust your path as needed. Reflection on past challenges and successes can inform current strategies, providing valuable lessons to enhance future endeavours.

Incorporating the SMART goal framework into different aspects of life can lead to significant personal growth. For those entering the workforce or balancing family responsibilities, setting career-related SMART goals can create a clear path toward professional development. Personal goals related to learning new skills, hobbies, or wellness improvements also benefit from this structured approach, turning aspirations into actionable plans.

For individuals recovering from past trauma, structured goal-setting facilitates healing and emotional resilience. By creating goals that promote self-care and personal well-being, individuals can gradually rebuild confidence and strength. For educators and mentors, teaching the art of goal-setting can equip others with tools to navigate life's complexities with a positive and proactive mindset.

Harnessing Creativity to Express and Explore Feelings

Creative expression serves as a powerful tool for emotional exploration. For women seeking to overcome insecurity or those healing from past trauma, engaging in artistic activities can be a transformative experience. Painting, writing, and dance provide emotional outlets that allow individuals to express feelings that may be challenging to articulate verbally. Through these creative processes, women can explore their inner world, uncover hidden emotions, and express themselves freely.

Artistic activities such as painting enable the expression of complex emotions through colours, shapes, and forms. For instance, when a woman applies paint to canvas, she creates a visual representation of her internal landscape. This not only allows her to make sense of her experiences but also brings a sense of release and relief. Similarly, writing offers a way to delve into thoughts and feelings, providing an opportunity to articulate experiences that might be difficult to share in conversation. Whether it's poetry, journaling, or narrative storytelling, writing encourages introspection and helps in organizing chaotic emotions into coherent stories.

Dance, too, plays an essential role in emotional exploration. It connects movement with emotion, allowing the physical body to express what words cannot. The rhythmic motion and expression involved in dance help participants release pent-up emotions and discover new perspectives on personal challenges. Dance can bridge the gap between mind and body, facilitating an emotional release that contributes to overall well-being.

Combining creativity with mindfulness enhances this emotional awareness even further. Mindfulness involves being present in the moment, which can deepen the connection to one's emotions during a creative process. For example, mindful painting encourages paying close attention to each brushstroke, colour choice, and feeling that arises. This practice fosters a deeper understanding of emotions and nurtures self-awareness. When women engage in creative tasks mindfully, they often find themselves more attuned to subtle emotions, leading to insights that promote healing and personal development.

Prompts can stimulate imagination and guide self-exploration. Writing prompts like "Describe a place where you feel truly at peace" or drawing exercises focused on illustrating one's current emotional state can unleash creativity while directing thought toward introspection. Such prompts act as catalysts, helping women break through creative blocks and revealing layers of their psyche they may have been unaware of. These exercises encourage women to explore aspects of their identity, beliefs, and desires in a safe and controlled manner.

Reflecting on creative outputs is another vital component of emotional exploration. By examining their artwork or written pieces after completion, women gain valuable insights into their personal experiences. Reflective practices involve asking questions about the themes, symbols, and emotions present in their work. What does the choice of colours in a painting reveal about current feelings? How do recurring themes in writing signify underlying issues? Reflection helps bridge the gap between unconscious thoughts and conscious understanding, offering a deeper comprehension of oneself.

Creative expression, combined with reflection, empowers women to understand their emotional responses and life events better. Art becomes a mirror reflecting true feelings and thoughts, while thoughtful analysis of creative work leads to a greater understanding of one's journey and growth.

Furthermore, engaging in these activities in a supportive environment can significantly enhance their benefits. Having a space free of judgment, whether it's a personal setting or a group workshop, allows women to express themselves honestly. Feedback from peers or facilitators can provide additional insights, while shared experiences foster a sense of community and belonging. When women feel supported in their creative endeavours, they are more likely to take risks, express vulnerability, and embrace their unique journeys without fear.

Meditation Practices for Inner Peace and Focus

Meditation is a powerful tool for cultivating inner peace and enhancing focus, providing women with a means to navigate their unique journeys with clarity and calmness. Among the most accessible meditation techniques are breath awareness and guided visualization, both of which can be seamlessly integrated into daily routines.

Breath awareness is fundamentally about anchoring your attention to the rhythmic flow of inhalations and exhalations. By simply focusing on each breath, you create a space where thoughts can come and go without judgment, easing the mind into a state of tranquillity. This practice helps in quieting the mental chatter that often accompanies stress and anxiety. You can start with just a few minutes a day, gradually increasing the duration as you become more comfortable with the practice.

Guided visualization, on the other hand, involves creating vivid mental images to promote relaxation and encourage positive thinking. Through this technique, you can mentally transport yourself to serene landscapes or imagine fulfilling experiences that evoke joy and serenity. Visualization serves as an anchor to pull focus away from distractions, allowing deeper immersion into peaceful states of mind. Engaging all senses during visualization—imagining sounds, smells, and sensations—enhances the experience and offers a more profound sense of escape and rejuvenation.

Mindfulness meditation stands out among these practices as a cornerstone for living in the present moment. By fostering an awareness of the present, mindfulness helps reduce anxiety by breaking the habit of dwelling on past tensions or future uncertainties. It encourages individuals to embrace life's moments fully, reducing stress and enhancing emotional resilience. Over time, practicing mindfulness can improve not only mental well-being but also physical health, as it has been linked to lower blood pressure and better sleep quality (Mayo Clinic Staff, 2023).

To truly benefit from meditation, establishing a personalized routine is essential. Just as one might schedule a workout or a meeting, carving out a specific time for meditation anchors it into your daily life. Consider starting with short sessions in the morning or evening when distractions are minimal. As you grow more accustomed to the practice, extend these sessions or integrate them at different times of the day, like during lunch breaks or before winding down at night. Consistency is key; maintaining a regular routine allows meditation's benefits to compound over time.

Despite its many advantages, some may find meditation challenging, especially in the beginning. It's common to encounter difficulties such as restlessness, impatience, or wandering thoughts. However, these challenges can be addressed by approaching meditation with curiosity and patience. Instead of striving for a perfect session, allow yourself to explore how your mind responds without criticism. Each distraction offers insight into your thought patterns and provides opportunities for growth. Embrace the process as a journey, recognizing that perfection isn't the goal; presence is.

For those interested in deepening their practice, attending meditation classes or utilizing apps designed specifically for meditation guidance can be valuable. These resources provide structured sessions led by experienced instructors, offering new techniques and community support. Such tools can help reinforce the practice while keeping motivation high through varied approaches and shared experiences.

Final Thoughts

In this chapter, we explored various transformative tools that empower personal development and foster self-discovery. Vision boards serve as a visual affirmation of individual aspirations, providing a creative way to focus on and achieve goals. Both physical and digital mediums for vision boards offer flexibility and adaptability, ensuring that they remain relevant as our dreams evolve. We also delved into the practice of journaling, which acts as a powerful method for reflection and allows individuals to gain insights into their emotions, thoughts, and life's trajectory. Consistent journaling aids in emotional processing and growth, offering a therapeutic outlet that enhances self-understanding and resilience.

Furthermore, we examined the significance of structured goal-setting, emphasizing how breaking down objectives into manageable steps can help maintain motivation and facilitate achievement. The SMART framework ensures clear and actionable goals that align with broader life values. Lastly, we discussed the healing potential of creativity and meditation, highlighting how engaging in artistic activities or mindfulness practices enables a deeper connection with oneself. These techniques promote emotional exploration and inner peace, which are crucial for overcoming challenges and embracing personal journeys with confidence. These paths collectively create a holistic framework for women to navigate their unique life experiences, fostering empowerment and self-esteem.

Fostering Joyful Relationships and Celebrating Authenticity

Fostering joyful relationships and celebrating authenticity are central to building a life filled with meaningful connections. At its core, this chapter delves into the journey of surrounding oneself with supportive individuals who nurture our true selves. Positive relationships form the foundation upon which self-esteem and happiness flourish, offering a safe haven where we can express our authentic selves without fear of judgment. Through nurturing environments, individuals find the courage for personal growth and exploration of identities. This sense of belonging is not only comforting but also transformative, as it empowers people to embrace their uniqueness and share it confidently with the world.

The chapter addresses the dual nature of relationships, emphasizing the importance of identifying both supportive and toxic influences in our lives. Readers will explore strategies for setting healthy boundaries without guilt, ensuring that their emotional well-being remains intact. The narrative includes techniques such as active listening and effective communication methods like using "I" statements, which help create genuine interactions rooted in mutual respect and empathy. Additionally, the text highlights the significance of participating in activities that spark happiness and offer restorative experiences. By incorporating these joyful practices, individuals can enrich their lives, contributing positively to their personal development while strengthening community ties. Throughout this exploration, readers will find insights into fostering environments where love and authenticity thrive, paving the way for collective fulfillment and empowerment.

Nurturing Supportive and Meaningful Relationships

Surrounding oneself with supportive individuals is a crucial component of fostering joyful relationships and embracing authenticity. Positive relationships play a significant role in our lives, serving as a foundation upon which self-esteem and overall happiness are built. When individuals are surrounded by a network of supportive people, they feel more confident in expressing their true selves, knowing that they are accepted and valued for who they are.

The transformative influence of positive relationships cannot be overstated. They act as a mirror reflecting back to us our worth and potential, instilling a sense of belonging and acceptance. This nurturing environment encourages personal growth by allowing individuals to explore their identities without fear of judgment or rejection. Studies have shown that people who engage in positive social interactions tend to experience higher levels of happiness and life satisfaction. By nurturing these relationships, we create a safe space where authenticity thrives, encouraging others to do the same.

Conversely, recognizing relationships that drain energy and hinder self-acceptance is critical in maintaining emotional well-being. Toxic relationships often manifest through continuous negativity, criticism, and a lack of genuine support. These relationships can lead to self-doubt and diminish one's confidence, making it challenging to embrace one's authentic self. Identifying toxic elements within relationships requires introspection and awareness of how certain interactions impact mental and emotional health. Once recognized, it becomes possible to set boundaries or distance oneself from such detrimental influences, paving the way for healthier connections.

Building deeper connections with loved ones emphasizes the importance of quality over quantity. In today's fast-paced world, it's easy to fall into the trap of valuing numerous superficial connections over meaningful interactions. However, the depth of a relationship significantly impacts its ability to support personal growth and authenticity. Investing time and effort into nurturing relationships allows individuals to develop strong bonds based on trust, mutual respect, and shared experiences. By prioritizing meaningful interactions, people can cultivate lasting connections that enrich their lives in profound ways.

One effective strategy for building deeper connections is practicing active listening. Active listening involves fully engaging with the speaker, paying attention to their words, tone, and non-verbal cues, and responding thoughtfully. It goes beyond merely hearing what someone is saying; it requires being present and showing genuine interest in their perspective. Through active listening, individuals demonstrate respect and empathy, reinforcing the value of the relationship. This practice not only strengthens the bond but also fosters an environment where authenticity is celebrated.

Moreover, active listening enhances communication, reducing misunderstandings and fostering a sense of understanding and support. When individuals feel heard and understood, they are more likely to open up and share their true thoughts and feelings, promoting a deeper connection. To practice active listening effectively, one can apply simple guidelines such as maintaining eye contact, avoiding interruptions, and providing feedback through nods or verbal affirmations. These small gestures can make a significant difference in creating meaningful conversations.

It's essential to approach relationships with an open heart and a willingness to invest time and emotion. While it may seem daunting at times, the rewards of forming genuine connections are immeasurable. By focusing on building and nurturing a supportive circle, individuals embark on a journey toward personal and mutual growth. In this interconnected web of relationships, everyone plays a vital role in supporting one another's authenticity, encouraging a culture of acceptance and growth.

Ultimately, surrounding ourselves with supportive individuals inspires us to become the best versions of ourselves. These relationships act as a safety net during challenging times and a source of joy and celebration during moments of achievement. By being intentional about the relationships we cultivate, we create a space where love, respect, and authenticity flourish. Through this process, we not only enhance our own lives but also contribute positively to the lives of those around us, fostering a collective sense of fulfillment and empowerment.

Communicating with Authenticity and Confidence

Empowering women to express their true thoughts and feelings confidently is vital in cultivating authentic connections and fostering self-assurance. The act of expressing one's true self invites a deeper understanding between individuals, strengthening personal and professional relationships. Authentic communication is the backbone of meaningful interactions; when we communicate genuinely, our words resonate more profoundly with others, fostering trust and respect.

When speaking from the heart, we bridge emotional and intellectual gaps, encouraging mutual empathy and support. The capacity to convey one's genuine emotions and thoughts reduces misunderstandings and conflicts, as it clears any ambiguities or assumptions that might arise in conversation. As more women embrace this honesty, they not only share their truths but also inspire others to do the same, creating a ripple effect that enhances the overall quality of discourse within communities.

Ensuring body language aligns with true feelings can greatly enhance non-verbal cues for authenticity. Non-verbal communication often conveys more than words alone, as gestures, facial expressions, and posture contribute significantly to how messages are perceived. When body language reflects genuine emotions, it strengthens verbal communication and reinforces credibility. For instance, maintaining eye contact and exhibiting open gestures while speaking conveys confidence and sincerity, making it easier for listeners to trust and engage with what is being said. Conversely, incongruence between spoken words and physical demeanour could lead to confusion or disbelief, undermining the speaker's message.

Thus, paying attention to aligning non-verbal cues with internal emotions can greatly enhance personal interactions. Being mindful of body language also empowers individuals to present themselves authentically, ensuring that their physical presence amplifies rather than hinders communication. This congruence becomes especially critical in settings where first impressions count, such as interviews or public speaking engagements, where every gesture can influence perception.

Practicing assertiveness is crucial in mastering the art of stating opinions and desires clearly. Assertiveness is about expressing personal viewpoints respectfully and firmly, without veering into aggression or passivity. It involves establishing a clear line of communication that respects both the speaker's and listener's rights. One effective guideline for practicing assertiveness begins with small steps in everyday situations, gradually building confidence and skill through practice.

For example, regularly asserting simple needs or preferences in low-pressure environments, like choosing a restaurant or scheduling activities, can serve as practical exercises. These early victories lay the foundation for addressing more significant matters confidently. Practicing assertiveness helps individuals gain confidence in their ability to express themselves in various contexts, ultimately enabling them to navigate both personal and professional landscapes with greater ease. Building these skills over time allows women to advocate for their needs, leading to more balanced and equitable exchanges in all areas of life.

Using "I" statements allows individuals to take personal ownership of their feelings and promotes clarity in communication. Constructing sentences from a first-person perspective—such as "I feel," "I need," or "I want"—encourages speakers to focus on their own emotions and experiences rather than projecting them onto others. This method avoids blame and fosters an environment where everyone involved can freely share their perspectives without fear of judgment or backlash.

For instance, saying, "I feel overwhelmed by the current workload," rather than "You're giving me too much work," invites others to understand your perspective and collaborate on solutions. This subtle shift in language emphasizes personal responsibility and accountability, making it easier for others to empathize and respond constructively. In essence, "I" statements nurture openness and understanding, paving the way for more honest and productive dialogue.

Setting Healthy Boundaries Without Guilt

Building joyful relationships and celebrating authenticity hinges on our ability to establish healthy boundaries effectively. Setting boundaries is not just a preventive measure but a foundational element for nurturing respectful and fulfilling relationships. It's important to understand what healthy boundaries are, why they matter, and how we can communicate them without guilt.

Healthy boundaries define what is acceptable in our relationships, serving as invisible lines that protect our emotional, physical, and psychological well-being. They help delineate where one person ends and another begins, allowing individuals to maintain a sense of self within their interactions. Without boundaries, people might feel overwhelmed or taken advantage of, which can lead to resentment and conflict. For example, agreeing to work overtime constantly, despite having other commitments, could result in burnout and strained personal connections.

Communicating boundaries effectively requires an understanding of one's own needs and the confidence to express them clearly. Many struggle with this because they fear coming across as difficult or demanding. However, it's crucial to remember that setting boundaries demonstrates self-respect and encourages a balanced dynamic. Communicating them doesn't have to be confrontational; it should be about asserting one's needs peacefully and confidently. A guideline for communicating boundaries is starting with "I" statements. For instance, saying, "I need some time each evening for myself to recharge," conveys your requirement without blaming others. Practicing assertiveness allows you to state your needs firmly but kindly.

To express needs without feeling guilty, it helps to keep in mind that everyone has limitations, and respecting those strengthens relationships. Recognizing that it's okay to prioritize your well-being is key. People often accept boundary violations out of guilt or the desire to please. Instead, framing requests positively and focusing on personal benefits can shift how boundaries are perceived. For instance, explaining that spending some alone time helps improve your mood and energy can make others more receptive to respecting your boundaries.

Recognizing signs of boundary violations is pivotal to maintaining healthy interactions. These violations might manifest as feelings of frustration, stress, or being overwhelmed. It's essential to stay attuned to these emotional cues as indicators that your limits may have been breached. An example would be feeling anxious every time a friend repeatedly calls during your work hours despite your earlier request for no interruptions. It's also important to acknowledge when someone attempts to manipulate, dismiss, or belittle your boundaries, as these are clear signs of disrespect. Regularly checking in on how certain interactions make you feel can help identify patterns and areas where boundaries might need reinforcement.

Reinforcing boundaries is not a one-time effort but an ongoing process. Life circumstances and relationship dynamics change, necessitating adjustments to ensure boundaries remain effective. To do so, regularly reflect on your needs and reassess if your boundaries align with your current situation. Encourage yourself to revisit and adjust boundaries as needed. This could involve renegotiating terms if previous arrangements become untenable due to new roles or responsibilities. For instance, if family obligations increase, you might need to communicate different availability times to colleagues.

The continual nature of reinforcing boundaries underscores the importance of adaptability in relationships. As trust and mutual respect grow, some boundaries may relax while others become stricter based on necessity and context. Open communication about these changes ensures transparency and prevents misunderstandings. Should breaches occur, it's beneficial to address them promptly. Expressing how certain behaviours impact you without assigning blame fosters constructive dialogue. An example could be informing a partner that frequent last-minute changes to shared plans create inconvenience and suggesting alternatives.

In some cases, reaching out for additional support can make navigating boundaries smoother, especially in complex power dynamics or emotionally charged situations. Engaging with a mentor, counsellor, or peer who has experience in setting boundaries can provide valuable insights and guidance. These professionals can offer strategies tailored to specific challenges, helping you navigate sensitive conversations or entrenched behaviour patterns. If difficulties persist, considering mediation or professional intervention might be necessary to facilitate deeper understanding and resolution.

Participating in Activities that Spark Happiness

Incorporating joy-inducing activities into daily life can significantly enhance overall well-being by promoting happiness and reducing stress. This begins with the exploration of personal interests and hobbies. Engaging in activities that elevate mood not only provides a sense of satisfaction but also serves as a tool to identify what truly brings joy. For example, creative pursuits like painting or crafting can evoke a deep sense of fulfillment, while outdoor activities such as hiking or gardening connect individuals with nature, offering both physical and emotional benefits.

Restorative activities—those that require little mental effort and provide a sense of "being away" from daily concerns—are particularly effective. According to Pressman et al. (2009), these activities maintain engagement and match an individual's interests and abilities, offering relief from routine pressures. Such activities might include nature walks, meditation, or even leisure travel, which are associated with improved psychological well-being and cognitive function.

However, many people face barriers that prevent them from participating in joyful activities. Time constraints, lack of motivation, or fear of trying something new often stand in the way. Overcoming these obstacles is essential for fostering joy. Setting aside specific time slots each week for leisure or breaking tasks into smaller, manageable steps can help mitigate time-related barriers. Building motivation might involve setting small goals or seeking inspiration from stories of others who have pursued similar paths successfully. For those dealing with fear, it's important to start with low-risk activities, gradually building comfort and confidence. Creating a supportive environment where one feels encouraged rather than judged helps in tackling these challenges.

Building connections through group engagement in joyful practices enhances the experience, adding a social element that strengthens community ties. Participating in group classes, clubs, or meetups focused on shared interests not only allows for skill development but also creates a network of like-minded individuals. For instance, joining a dance class or a book club can create meaningful relationships, fostering a sense of belonging and support. These interactions provide a platform for sharing experiences and learning from one another, enhancing the joy derived from the activities themselves.

An essential yet often overlooked aspect of cultivating joy is keeping a journal or record of happy moments. Documenting experiences that bring happiness serves as a powerful reminder of what to pursue when times feel challenging. Reflecting on these joyful experiences through writing or photography can provide inspiration and motivate continued engagement in such activities. While this practice may seem simple, it can be transformative, encouraging individuals to focus on positive emotions and valuable experiences.

Furthermore, research suggests that engaging in diverse, enjoyable leisure activities contributes to both psychological and physiological health benefits. The Pittsburgh Enjoyable Activities Test (PEAT) found that participation in various types of leisure activities correlates with lower blood pressure and stress markers, improving overall perceptions of physical function and positive psychosocial states (Pressman et al., 2009). Thus, integrating a variety of enjoyable activities into one's lifestyle not only enhances mood but promotes long-term health outcomes.

Joyful activities do more than just entertain; they serve as critical components of a fulfilling life. For women balancing multiple responsibilities, identifying these pockets of joy can be especially empowering. Reconnecting with forgotten passions or discovering new interests can offer rejuvenation amidst daily demands. Similarly, for individuals recovering from trauma, exploring joy can be a form of self-care that aids healing and builds resilience. Activities that promote creativity, relaxation, and connection act as "restorers," replenishing depleted resources and nurturing emotional well-being.

Educators, mentors, and counsellors can also harness the power of joy-inducing activities as tools for supporting those they guide. Recommending such activities as part of personal development programs can have profound effects, fostering environments where individuals feel supported in their pursuit of happiness. Encouraging clients or students to explore various interests not only builds confidence but provides opportunities for growth and collaboration.

Creating a culture where joyful engagement is valued requires intentional action. Communities and organizations can play a role by facilitating access to resources, creating safe spaces for exploration, and recognizing the importance of leisure in enhancing quality of life. By prioritizing joy and understanding its impact, we foster environments where everyone can thrive, celebrating authenticity and building meaningful connections along the way.

Celebrating Personal Milestones and Achievements

Celebrating personal achievements plays a crucial role in nurturing self-worth and motivation. By recognizing even the smallest of victories, individuals can enhance their sense of accomplishment and well-being, in a world that often emphasizes grand success, taking time to appreciate smaller achievements helps to set personal milestones. These milestones are not confined to monumental events; rather, they include the small steps that contribute to our growth and development.

Defining these personal milestones begins by acknowledging that achievements come in varying sizes. What may seem trivial to one person might hold significant meaning to another. For instance, finishing a project, making healthy lifestyle choices for a week, or overcoming a personal fear are all milestones worth noting. Understanding this broad spectrum of achievement allows us to acknowledge progress in all its forms, reinforcing that every step forward is significant. This perspective fosters a mindset where individuals feel valued for who they are rather than only celebrating when they reach major goals.

Creating meaningful rituals for celebration is an effective way to commemorate accomplishments. Whether it's through writing about achievements in a journal, sharing your success with friends, or indulging in a small treat as a reward, establishing these practices makes the celebration more tangible. Rituals don't have to be complex; they simply need to reflect personal values and the significance of the achievement being celebrated. These practices reinforce the value of accomplishment and serve as reminders of one's capabilities. Establishing such rituals is a powerful way to recognize success and sustain motivation over time.

Reflecting on the effort invested in achieving goals cultivates gratitude and pride. It's easy to overlook the hard work and dedication behind an achievement, but recognizing the journey enhances the value of the outcome. When individuals take the time to consider the challenges they overcame and the perseverance required, they build a deeper appreciation for their efforts. This reflection not only boosts self-esteem but also encourages a positive attitude toward future endeavours. By appreciating the journey and acknowledging the hurdles faced, we prepare ourselves for continued growth and resilience.

It is essential to celebrate progress rather than perfection. Many people fall into the trap of waiting for the perfect moment or result before they allow themselves to celebrate. However, this mindset overlooks the beauty of incremental progress. Embracing imperfections in achievements highlights the importance of learning and growth over flawlessness. Every step taken toward a goal, despite setbacks or mistakes, is worthy of acknowledgment. Celebrating these moments encourages a culture of resilience and continuous improvement, which is far more sustainable and fulfilling than striving for unattainable perfection.

The act of celebrating itself has psychological benefits. Research has shown that acknowledging small achievements releases dopamine, a neurotransmitter associated with pleasure and motivation (*Celebrate the Small Stuff*, n.d.). This chemical response reinforces positive behaviour and motivates individuals to pursue further accomplishments. The feeling of joy and satisfaction experienced during celebration encourages the repetition of the behaviours that led to success, creating a positive cycle of achievement and recognition.

Furthermore, recording progress regularly can amplify the

effects of celebrating achievements. As noted by Harvard Business School researchers, maintaining a record of daily successes can significantly boost motivation. Documenting these wins, no matter how minor they may seem, helps consolidate them in memory and increases confidence (Mind Tools Content Team, 2022). This practice not only aids in reflecting on how far one has come but also serves as a motivational tool during times of doubt or challenge.

For women seeking guidance, particularly those balancing professional and personal responsibilities, recognizing personal achievements can serve as a foundation for building self-esteem and combating insecurity. By focusing on what has been accomplished rather than what remains unmet, individuals empower themselves to see their own worth more clearly. This shift in perspective is especially beneficial for women who juggle diverse roles and face societal pressures.

Individuals recovering from trauma can also find healing in celebrating achievements. Recognizing progress in overcoming emotional obstacles, no matter the size, can foster resilience. Celebrations of small victories remind them of their strength and capacity for growth, aiding recovery and enhancing emotional well-being.

Educators and mentors play a vital role in fostering this practice among their students or mentees. By encouraging them to commemorate both academic and personal milestones, they instill a habit of self-appreciation that contributes to long-term success. Providing a supportive environment where achievements, big and small, are acknowledged helps individuals develop a robust sense of self-worth that transcends external validation.

Wrapping Up

In this chapter, we delved into the essence of building meaningful connections and embracing our true selves across all dimensions of life. We explored how surrounding oneself with supportive people can pave the way for personal growth and authenticity. The importance of recognizing and nurturing positive relationships was emphasized, as they serve as a mirror reflecting our self-worth and potential. These networks provide a safe haven, allowing individuals to express their true selves without fear of judgment. On the other hand, identifying and setting boundaries with toxic influences is crucial to maintaining emotional well-being. By focusing on quality over quantity in our interactions, we create deep, lasting bonds capable of enriching our lives profoundly.

Furthermore, we highlighted the power of active listening as a strategy to foster deeper connections, enhance communication and promote authenticity within relationships. Being fully present and engaging with others reinforces the value of genuine dialogue, paving the way for mutual understanding and empathy. By approaching relationships with openness and a willingness to invest time and emotion, individuals embark on a journey toward shared growth and fulfillment. Prioritizing these authentic interactions enables us to cultivate supportive circles that not only enhance personal happiness but also contribute positively to the overall fabric of our communities.

Conclusion

As you close this book, take a moment to reflect on the changes you've embraced. This journey may have started as a quest for guidance and support, but it has evolved into something far more profound—a personal revolution of growth, resilience, and self-love. Remember the moments of doubt that once weighed heavily on your spirit, now transformed into stepping stones leading to newfound strength. Reflect on how each chapter has contributed uniquely to this metamorphosis, offering insights and tools that have empowered you to rebuild your relationship with yourself and the world around you.

Pause for a minute and think about the strength you have discovered within yourself, the type of strength you didn't recognize before. It might be resilience in the face of adversity or the fresh courage to pursue paths once deemed unattainable. Whatever form your strength takes, acknowledge it. You are a mosaic of strength and resilience; with every challenge you face, you have added a piece to this beautiful masterpiece of who you are. Your development doesn't just end with understanding; it thrives in action—the actions you've taken to assert your worth, build your confidence, and embrace your individuality.

Now, let us reaffirm those strengths. What qualities can you now list about yourself that perhaps went unnoticed before?

Consider taking a moment to put pen to paper and write them down. You might find that these are not merely characteristics but accomplishments that have together paved the path for empowerment and joy. These attributes echo your self-worth and signal the confidence that resides in you. They serve as reminders that beneath any lingering insecurity lies undeniable greatness waiting to emerge fully.

Personal growth doesn't end here. It's an ongoing journey— a dynamic process where each day brings new opportunities for unfolding potential. Picture yourself one year from today, envisioning the new heights you can reach by continuing to nurture your authentic self. Consider setting new goals that align with your core values and aspirations, whether personal, professional or within your community. Allow yourself to dream boldly, chase those dreams with conviction, and hold on to the knowledge that you possess everything needed to turn them into reality.

Think about the people in your life who uplift you. Nurturing positive influences and building supportive relationships are crucial for continued empowerment. Surround yourself with individuals who celebrate your successes, understand your challenges, and inspire you to rise beyond them. Make a conscious commitment to invest time and energy in these connections. Just like flowers in a well-tended garden, relationships blossom when cultivated with care, compassion, and genuine appreciation. Together, you can inspire one another's journeys and experience the shared joy of thriving collectively.

In moving forward, embrace and celebrate your unique qualities and experiences. Authenticity is not only a source of strength but also the embodiment of empowerment. Now, think, how can you share this distinct light with the world? Celebrate it in ways that resonate deeply with your spirit. Appreciate the nuances that make you, well, you. Your uniqueness is your superpower—an extraordinary blend of traits, perspectives, and talents that only you can bring to the table. Share this gift openly, letting others bask in its brilliance while drawing strength and encouragement from it themselves.

This entire experience—this transformative voyage—is a testament to your resilience and capacity for growth. It serves as a reminder that healing is possible, confidence is attainable, and self-love is paramount in shaping the life you deserve. Each step you've taken through these pages is a declaration of your determination to heal past traumas, break free from self-doubt, and craft an identity defined by purpose and passion. By reaching out for help, exploring methods of personal development, and committing to change, you've begun crafting a legacy of empowerment that will impact not just your life but also the lives of those who look to you for inspiration.

As you venture into tomorrow's challenges, carry with you the lessons learned and the wisdom gained. Embrace this new chapter of your life with enthusiasm and hope. Continue to seek opportunities for learning, growth, and transformation, knowing that uncertainty is simply another canvas for creation. Every obstacle becomes surmountable when viewed through the lens of possibility. Trust in your ability to navigate life's complexities, fortified by the knowledge and insight acquired on this journey.

Consider revisiting these pages whenever reminders of your capability and worth are needed. Let this book serve as a companion—one that champions your progress and reignites your passion for further exploration. Even when not actively reading, know that its spirit accompanies you, infusing your days with motivation and encouragement.

Finally, remember that your story is yours to tell. It is shaped by your choices, nurtured by your perseverance, and enriched by your experiences. As the author of your narrative, wield your pen with intention and creativity. Write chapters filled with fulfillment, compassion, and purpose. Inspire others with your authenticity, leaving behind a legacy of hope and strength for future generations. And never forget that within you resides an infinite potential to create, empower, and transcend.

You stand poised now at the edge of endless possibilities, ready to leave behind shadows of insecurity and step fully into the brilliance of your being. Celebrate the completion of this chapter and the exciting new ones yet to come. You have embarked on a powerful journey—one of healing, discovery, and boundless potential. Know that wherever your path leads, it is illuminated by the enduring flame of your inner light. Shine brightly, journey onward, and continue to become the magnificent person you are destined to be.

Please Leave A Review!

Dear Reader,

If you enjoyed this book, please consider leaving a review on Amazon.

Thank You!

References

1. Ackerman, C. (2018, May 23). *What Is Self-Esteem? a Psychologist Explains.* PositivePsychology.com. https://posi tivepsychology.com/self-esteem/

2. *Coping with Peer Pressure: Building Resilience & Self-Confidence | Therapy for Young Adults | Therapy for Colorado.* (n.d.). Two Rivers Therapy & Consulting. https://www.twor iverstherapycolorado.com/blog/coping-with-peer-pressure-strategies-for-building-resilience-and-self-confidence

3. Geall, L. (2020, February 16). *External validation: why do I need everyone to like me?* Stylist. https://www.stylist.co.uk/life/ external-validation-self-esteem-taylor-swift-miss-americana -how-to-improve-internal-validation/356826

4. Kim, J., Kwon, J. H., Kim, J., Kim, E. J., Kim, H. E., Kyeong, S., & Kim, J.-J. (2021, July 21). *The Effects of Positive or Negative self-talk on the Alteration of Brain Functional Connectivity by Performing Cognitive Tasks.* Scientific Reports. https://doi.or g/10.1038/s41598-021-94328-9

5. Liu, Q., Jiang, M., Li, S., & Yang, Y. (2021, January 29). *Social support, resilience, and self-esteem protect against common mental health problems in early adolescence*. Medicine. https://www.ncbi.nlm.nih.gov/pmc/articles/PMC7850671/

6. Pascoe, G. (2023, March 21). *The Value in Finding and Using Your Strengths | Mentorloop*. Mentorloop Mentoring Software. https://mentorloop.com/blog/using-your-strengths/

7. *Self-Confidence Versus Self-Esteem*. (2015). Psychology Today. https://www.psychologytoday.com/us/blog/hide-and-seek/201510/self-confidence-versus-self-esteem

8. Strong, S. (2014). *Simply Strong*. Simply Strong. https://www.simplystrongteams.com/identify-strengths-exercise

9. *The Trap of External Validation for Self-Esteem*. (2017, August 28). Psych Central. https://psychcentral.com/blog/psychology-self/2017/08/validation-self-esteem

10. *The Power of Self-Talk: Boosting Confidence and Performance*. (n.d.). Accelerate.uofuhealth.utah.edu. https://accelerate.uofuhealth.utah.edu/leadership/the-power-of-self-talk-boosting-confidence-and-performance

11. Conway, S.-M. (2024, January 30). *A Gratitude Meditation to Relieve Anxiety*. Mindfulness Exercises. https://mindfulnessexercises.com/an-anti-anxiety-gratitude-practice/

12. Gupta, S. (2024, March 22). *25 self-love affirmations to remind you of your worth*. Verywell Mind. https://www.verywellmind.com/25-self-love-affirmations-8553223

13. How to Stop Comparing Yourself to Others. (2018). Psychology Today. https://www.psychologytoday.com/intl/blog/prescriptions-for-life/201803/how-to-stop-comparing-yourself-to-others

14. LCSW, O. A. (2023, April 26). *How to Make Positive Affirmations That Actually Work for You.* Wondermind. https://www.wondermind.com/article/positive-affirmations/

15. Mayo Clinic Staff. (2020, September 15). *Mindfulness exercises.* Mayo Clinic. https://www.mayoclinic.org/healthy-lifestyle/consumer-health/in-depth/mindfulness-exercises/art-20046356

16. Peartree, A. (2017, June 13). *Overcoming Envy: How to Stop Feeling Inferior and Insecure.* Tiny Buddha. https://tinybuddha.com/blog/overcoming-envy-stop-feeling-inferior-bad/

17. Raypole, C. (2020, November 13). *Emotional triggers: Definition and how to manage them.* Healthline. https://www.healthline.com/health/mental-health/emotional-triggers

18. University, T. (n.d.). *Growth Mindset: Celebrating Failures.* Www.touro.edu. https://www.touro.edu/departments/cetl/blog/growth-mindset-celebrating-failures-.php

19. Young, T. (n.d.). *Success and Failure: How Growth Mindset Can Change Education.* Blog.mindresearch.org. https://blog.mindresearch.org/blog/how-growth-mindset-can-change-education

20. jaceylenae. (2020, February 18). *How To Manage Social Media FOMO, Jealousy & Anxiety - Damsel In Dior*. Damsel in Dior - a Fashion, Travel & Lifestyle Blog. https://dam selindior.com/how-to-manage-social-media-fomo-jealousy-anxiety/

21. Chowdhury, M. R. (2019, April 9). *The Neuroscience of Gratitude and Effects on the Brain*. PositivePsychology.com. https://positivepsychology.com/neuroscience-of-gratitude/

22. *Embrace Your Imperfections*. (2021). Psychology Today. https://www.psychologytoday.com/intl/blog/conquering-co dependency/202102/embrace-your-imperfections

23. *Here's Why Accepting Your Imperfections Can Help You Find Meaning in Life*. (n.d.). Happify.com. https://www.happify.co m/hd/accepting-your-imperfections-can-help-you-find-mea ning-in-life/

24. *How to deal with emotional pain: 8 ways to support yourself*. (n.d.). Calm Blog. https://www.calm.com/blog/emotional-pa in

25. Johns Hopkins Medicine. (2019). *Forgiveness: Your Health Depends on It*. Johns Hopkins Medicine. https://www.hopkin smedicine.org/health/wellness-and-prevention/forgiveness-your-health-depends-on-it

26. *Key Insights into the Psychology of Forgiveness | Resiliency*. (2024, June 21). Resiliency Clinic. https://resiliencyclinic.com/ the-psychology-of-forgiveness

27. *Mantra: A Powerful Way to Improve Your Well-Being*. (2019). Psychology Today. https://www.psychologytoday.com/intl/b log/living-forward/201906/mantra-powerful-way-improve-your-well-being

28. Parry, G. (2024, July 29). *Embracing Personal Mantras and Positive Self-Talk - Global Services In Education*. Global Services

in Education. https://www.gsineducation.com/blog/embraci
ng-personal-mantras-and-positive-self-talk

29. Reid, S. (2022, June 6). *Gratitude: The Benefits and How to
Practice It - HelpGuide.org*. HelpGuide.org. https://www.helpg
uide.org/mental-health/wellbeing/gratitude

30. *The Importance of Self-Compassion in Mental Health
Recovery*. (2024, August 21). Premier Psychiatric Services.
https://premierpsychtn.com/2024/08/21/the-importance-o
f-self-compassion-in-mental-health-recovery/

31. *How To Make A Vision Board: 2023 Step-By-Step Guide*.
(n.d.). Milanote. https://milanote.com/guide/vision-board

32. *How Creative Arts Therapy Benefits Teens - Sedona Sky
Academy*. (2024). Sedonasky.org. https://www.sedonasky.org/
blog/arts-therapy-benefits-teens

33. *How to write SMART goals [with examples]*. (2024).
Getguru.com. https://www.getguru.com/reference/smart-g
oals

34. Koschalk, K. (2023, October 24). *Journaling for Personal
Growth: The Impact of Journaling for Self-Improvement*. Rose-
bud.app; Rosebud. https://www.rosebud.app/blog/journalin
g-for-personal-growth

35. Mayo Clinic Staff. (2023, December 14). *Meditation: A
simple, fast way to reduce stress*. Mayo Clinic. https://www.m
ayoclinic.org/tests-procedures/meditation/in-depth/meditat
ion/art-20045858

36. Mayo Clinic Staff. (2020, September 15). *Mindfulness
exercises*. Mayo Clinic. https://www.mayoclinic.org/healthy-
lifestyle/consumer-health/in-depth/mindfulness-exercises/a
rt-20046356

37. Perry, E. (2023, June 15). *5 steps to create a vision board that
does its job*. BetterUp. https://www.betterup.com/blog/how-

to-create-vision-board

38. Sudarshan Somanathan. (2024, November 6). *How to Find the Right Accountability Partner for Your Goals.* ClickUp. https://clickup.com/blog/accountability-partner/

39. Sutton, J. (2018, May 14). *5 Benefits of Journaling for Mental Health.* Positive Psychology. https://positivepsychology.com/benefits-of-journaling/

40. Zimmermann, N., & Mangelsdorf, H. H. (2020, September). *Emotional benefits of brief creative movement and art interventions.* The Arts in Psychotherapy. https://doi.org/10.1016/j.aip.2020.101686

41. *Celebrate the small stuff.* (n.d.). Extension.umn.edu. https://extension.umn.edu/two-you-video-series/celebrate-small-stuff

42. Larsen, A. (2024, February 20). *The Importance of Love on Well-Being.* My Best Self 101. https://www.mybestself101.org/blog/the-importance-of-love-on-wellbeing

43. Mind Tools Content Team. (2022). *MindTools | Home.* Www.mindtools.com. https://www.mindtools.com/ax3c2aw/celebrating-achievement

44. Mayo Clinic Staff. (2020, May 29). *Being assertive: Reduce stress, communicate better.* Mayo Clinic. https://www.mayoclinic.org/healthy-lifestyle/stress-management/in-depth/assertive/art-20044644

45. Northwestern Medicine Staff. (2021, September). *5 Benefits of Healthy Relationships.* Northwestern Medicine; Northwestern Medicine. https://www.nm.org/healthbeat/healthy-tips/5-benefits-of-healthy-relationships

46. Odell, C. A. (n.d.). *How is life tree(ting) you?: Trust, safety, and respect - the importance of boundaries | student affairs.* Studentaffairs.stanford.edu. https://studentaffairs.stanford.ed

u/how-life-treeting-you-importance-of-boundaries

47. Pressman, S. D., Matthews, K. A., Cohen, S., Martire, L. M., Scheier, M., Baum, A., & Schulz, R. (2009, September). *Association of Enjoyable Leisure Activities With Psychological and Physical Well-Being.* Psychosomatic Medicine. https://doi.org/10.1097/psy.0b013e3181ad7978

48. Reid, S. (2022, July 6). *Setting Healthy Boundaries in Relationships - HelpGuide.org.* HelpGuide.org. https://www.helpguide.org/relationships/social-connection/setting-healthy-boundaries-in-relationships

49. *The Power of Assertiveness: A Woman's Guide to Expressing Herself Confidently.* (2024, March 20). Rapoport Psychological Services 2021. https://www.rapoportpsychological.com/therapy-blog/the-power-of-assertiveness-a-womans-guide-to-expressing-herself-confidently

50. Tan, C.-Y., Chuah, C.-Q., Lee, S.-T., & Tan, C.-S. (2021, July 6). *Being Creative Makes You Happier: the Positive Effect of Creativity on Subjective Well-Being.* International Journal of Environmental Research and Public Health. https://doi.org/10.3390/ijerph18147244

www.ingramcontent.com/pod-product-compliance
Lightning Source LLC
Chambersburg PA
CBHW031315250726